a walk around
DUBLIN

a walk around DUBLIN

Vincent Caprani

Appletree Press

To my mother and in
memory of my late father,
who together enriched our boyhood with
happy walkabouts, merry songs and vivid tales.

Published and printed by
The Appletree Press Ltd
19–21 Alfred Street
Belfast BT2 8DL
1992

The author wishes to express his gratitude to Feargal Quinn of Superquinn Ltd, and to the editor of IRELAND *OF THE WELCOMES* magazine for permission to use previously published material.

British Library Cataloguing-in-Publication Data
A catalogue record for this book is
available from the British Library.

ISBN 0 86281 343 3

9 8 7 6 5 4 3 2 1

Contents

Introduction

I DON'T think anyone can be said to know Dublin. The best anyone can claim is that he or she knows something of it, for there are several Dublins, in fact. If, like me, you enjoy studying old maps and prints of the city, then you'll probably recognise how complex is the question: 'What is Dublin?' New areas are constantly being added, enlarged and superimposed on older areas, one after another, and they don't necessarily coincide. Nor do our impressions of the inhabitants – or what's often termed 'the real characters' – necessarily coincide.

Can the maritime suburbs of Howth, Sandymount or Dun Laoghaire, for instance, be deemed part of Dublin? Certainly, if we mean 'County' Dublin. I comfort myself with the observation that if the place holds a special charm, legend or childhood memory, then it's part of my Dublin.

Yet, to judge by the number of books published, and the lists of second-hand books dealing with Dublin, it might seem that only a fool would want to add to the catalogue. Be that as it may, I also take comfort from the fact that someone once said it's a wise fool who knows his own folly. And to the student of history – and even to those of us who are neither wise nor anxious to give so grand a title to our natural curiosity about our town, its people and its tales – there can be few greater pleasures than lacing up a good pair of walking boots, slipping pen and notebook in pocket and going for a stroll.

Such strolls are often a kind of persistent questing for our own personal identity as well as for the identities of other Dubliners, past and present. It is not easy to say why, on such peregrinations, a sense of history matters, but it unquestionably does. It imparts a feeling of wonder and of distant history being as close as yesterday. Many of the Dubliners whom we are sure to meet on such strolls –

certainly a fair number of my generation and beyond – will have maintained a curious detachment from today's feverish chase after innovation and modernity. What difference will today, or any day, make in the enormous sequence of the seasons? Why, in Spencer's words:

> . . . speed today, to be put back tomorrow
> To feed on hope, to pine with fear and sorrow . . .

Why speed, when tomorrow will be a day just like this, when nothing much will have changed – and yet when so much is changing – when tomorrow, and the day after it, is surely another day nearer to the last day?

It is the yesterdays, not the tomorrows, that really matter and that bind us to our mother town.

12
13

· 1 ·

The Quays

ALL civilisation starts by a riverside. Dublin, like a thousand other towns, grew up on a river because of the importance of water as a highway. Or rather, Dublin grew to maturity on three rivers, for the city is situated at the terminal point where the Liffey, the Dodder and the Tolka empty into a bay which is reckoned to be about six miles in length and five and a half in width, give or take a foam-crested wave or two. These rivers (not to mention the subterranean and largely forgotten Camac, Poddle and Bradoge streams) cut and carve their mark upon the people they foster just as surely as they incise their marks upon the land itself.

One of my recent saunters down by the docks was enriched by a casual encounter with a square-jawed septuagenarian in a cloth cap and a blue gansey who (if I'd taken the trouble to ask his name) would, I feel, have inevitably answered 'Jem' or 'Whacker' or 'Nedser'. Or perhaps he might have had an even more colourful nickname, for Ringsend may justifiably claim to be the world capital of nicknames and sobriquets, and one of its pubs, the Oarsman, proudly displays on its wall, like a museum show-piece, a long and hallowed list of more than 500 local nicknames. The man in the cap and gansey was gazing across the river – perhaps into the past? – when I came upon him and engaged him in conversation. It didn't take long to discover that he wasn't overly impressed by the new Toll Bridge, nor the Point Depot 'with all them shaggin' rock-an'-roll bands', nor (back down by the Custom House Dock) the impressive skyline of the new International Financial Services Centre complex – 'shaggin' Yuppy skyscraper, givin' the town notions above herself and pretendin' to be more important than she is. 'Clare to God you'd find more elegance in a whore's handbag!' Thereafter he talked movingly of a time when the entire river as far as Butt Bridge was crowded with pert little steamers, the odd four-master, lumpy cargo boats, colliers, freighters, and tugs fussing and hooting and nursing their charges home to berth. 'Vast quantities of everyday merchandise, there was: meat, tea, coffee, sugar, wool, timber, coal, cattle, horses, you name it! – all of it comin' and goin' through them docks. An' fruit an' veggibles from the tropics, and wine and beer barrels. It was a place of sweet scents and sour smells in them days.'

'Twas also a richly coloured tale of industry spiced with adventure, for the crowded waterway in his time was the commencement and the termination of enterprises which reached the ends of the earth. 'Shure, sailors from all over the world knew the Pigeon House and Bull lighthouses better nor they knew their own heathen jungles', he added with evident pride. He rattled off statistics too: 'Sixty-two cranes, 'cludin' the one-hundred-ton job at the North Wall Extension, an' with berthage of just under 20,000 feet and four miles of water frontage.'

And did he have any amusing yarns?

'Oh many, I can tell ya! But the best of all is in me grandfather's time – or maybe it was the grandfather's oul fellah? – anyway, them oul-timers like meself an' me father an' all of us hereabouts was dockers and rivermen from way back. No matter a damn, it was a long time ago in the last centr'y when the first-ever cargo of huge ice blocks was brung inta Dublin port. Now, yeh must remember that this new commodity was such a rarity in them days – back in the 1850s or thereabouts – that it appeared on nobody's list or schedule, an' because of the confusion, it was quickly unloaded above at the Custom House Dock and left to the clerical Johnnies to sort the matter out. Meanwhile the officials were debatin' be letter 'tween here and London whether it was raw or manufactured material. At long last it was classified as dry goods, an' be the time the whole argument was concluded the ice had completely melted away inta the Liffey an' gone out with the tide', he chuckled.

He'd been a docker all his life until, in the 1970s, man-power was replaced by mechanisation. Gone are the teeming gangs of carters, dockers, stevedores, bargees, lightermen and crane-drivers. 'The place is a graveyard now', he sighed. 'I seldom come down here anymore.' He politely declined my invitation to continue the chat over a pint in MacDermott's. And when I reluctantly bid him farewell he nodded affably and then returned his melancholy gaze to the Liffey's dark water. I turned back once, waving my hand, and – so typical of such riverside folk who'd spent a lifetime waving a blessing to outgoing voyagers and welcoming incomers – he doffed his old cloth cap and held it aloft like a pennon until both of us were almost out of sight. When I sneaked a final glance over my shoulder I glimpsed an old man limping slowly away from me and down the quay, seawards, someone steeped in the lost wonder of youth and the pageantry of a once-proud river.

For my part, as I trudged up the quays, inland and landlubber fashion, I thought that Nature never intended the Liffey to be anything more than a not-too-deep salmon stream. Upriver, at Islandbridge and Leixlip (the latter from the Norse word for salmon, 'lax', and 'leap'), encouraged my musings. Also, a shipping report of 1590 gives the depth of the river between what is now Wood and Upper Ormand quays as varying between three feet and six feet, yet this small depth was apparently considered satisfactory for those days. This is, of course, at a time when the tangle of dynastic disputes, Drake and Raleigh's voyages and nascent empire-building, religious rivalries and sectarian struggles, burgeoning commerce, and the ongoing wars against Irish chieftains like the Great O'Neill caused Good Queen Bess to write to her Lord Deputy Mountjoy that 'Dublin standing so commodiously, is a Port not to be overthrown'!

Our little salmon stream was now an integral part of European power politics. Perhaps it always had been? The Liffey, and the port that stands at its mouth, has more than twenty centuries of history associated with it. Ever since the days when Phoenician and Milesian traders made their way to the wooded banks of Anna Livia to exchange their Mediterranean wares for tin and gold, and when Ptolemy (a century and a half before the Christian era) recorded the existence of the city Eblana, the Liffeyside has been part of the European story. The estuary has seen many strange and stirring sights since Ptolemy's days. It has heard the keels of fierce Viking raiders crash onto its sands and witnessed many a bloody conflict before the Norse won the right to erect the Steyne, a symbolic high stone signifying victory and possession which stood for 900 years at what is now the junction of Townsend Street and Hawkins Street.

There was further bloodshed along its creeks and across the river fords when the warrior king Brian Boru (Ireland's Charlemagne) finally curbed Danish power in 1014. Though severely chastised at Clontarf, the Norsemen returned to hold sway over most of the eastern seaboard. They were the first to commence the work of making dock and harbour accommodation. As late as 1177 the old Danish bridge – probably the first to span the Liffey – still stood, and up to it the Viking ships came to discharge their cargoes and to take back to Scandinavia the merchandise or collected plunder from the surrounding countryside. Across that same narrow wooden bridge, in 1170, the Norse-Dubliners were sent scurrying after their first bloody encounter with a new and more formidable breed of invader: the mounted and mail-clad Norman knight with his phalanx of deadly longbow men. Vanquished and banished to the north bank of the river, they were permitted by the new overlords to settle on land soon to be known as Oxmantown (derived from Ostman, or Eastman, a name given to all Norsemen originating from the east of Dublin).

The new invaders lost no time in sailing their own fleets up the estuary; soon a brisk and lucrative trade was opened up with fellow Normans at Bristol and at other cross-channel ports. St Werburgh's Church is an interesting reminder of that Bristol connection. Werburgha, a Saxon princess and nun who died in 683, was patroness of a church in Bristol, and King Henry II, wary of the sudden political power and prestige of his Norman lords by the Liffey, granted the city of Dublin by charter of 1172 'to the men of Bristol'. The earliest printed account of the port of Dublin was that written by Gerard Boate in 1649, at which period there was only six feet of water at the bar at low tide, and vessels drawing five feet could get no further up the river than Ringsend, where they became stranded at low tide. No man-made embankments channelled Anna Livia in those days. For centuries the tide flowed up to the muddy tracks leading down to, or lining, the river. This was the strand. Dubliners called it so. The name still survives in Little Strand Street and Great Strand Street running parallel to the river from Arran Street to Liffey Street, and it is difficult for us to realise now (when four or five miles of land occupy a space where once the sea flowed) that the coastline ran from Ballybough to Amiens Street, Beresford Place, Strand Street and Capel Street Bridge.

As time went on and the size of ships increased, the estuary presented a problem of growing perplexity. The waterway was silting up with a dangerous bar and with shoals that increased in size each year. Prior to the eighteenth century the larger ships were in the habit of anchoring in the bay, near Dalkey, and discharging their cargoes into lighter craft for conveyance to the city. So difficult was the problem that the virtual abandonment of the Liffey as a practicable port was under serious consideration. Some were even suggesting alternative harbours – Howth, Dun Laoghaire, Sandycove – with connecting canals to bring the goods into the city. The city fathers decided that they would have to deepen the river, dredge it and channel it. By 1710 we hear reports of dredging and procuring vast quantities of stone and faggots to wall the channel in, and the laying of 'kishes' filled with stone and backed by sand and gravel. The North and the South walls were built and later extended.

Meanwhile, Dublin had been graced with the first of today's familiar quays: Ormond Quay. Credit for this innovation, which was to have such an important bearing on the future development of the city, must go to the Duke of Ormond, the viceroy who did so much to alter Dublin from a decaying medieval township into what was shortly to become 'the second city of the Empire'. When the duke was shown Sir Humphrey Jervis's plans for the development of a section of the northside river bank, he noticed that the rears of the houses and warehouses were facing onto the river and that the river embankment contained no wall. Ormond persuaded Jervis to 'reverse' the houses so that their fronts looked out onto the river. He also suggested the interposition of a stone quay. Jervis, already in trouble with the Corporation and needing the influence of a powerful patron, took the hint and duly obliged. Thus, Ormond's aestheticism and farsightedness initiated the entire system of quays, and the attractiveness of that first quay was soon extended downriver as Bachelor's Walk, a riparian promenade affording pleasant views across the Liffey towards Trinity College. Soon afterwards, however, the south-bank landlords, lessees and magnates – St George Usher, Henry Aston et al – caught the bug and quickly followed suit. Not to be outdone, their northside counterparts – the Earl of Arran (a younger son of Ormond), William Eden (Lord Auckland) and William Ellis – joined the fray in a contest 'for the advantage, ornament and beauty of the city'. Not all were landowners or lessees: Burgh Quay commemorates Colonel Tom Burgh, an architect who, in 1707, was one of the first to advocate improvements to the harbour; amongst his many excellent suggestions was the necessity of enquiring into 'what sort of bottom there is, whether it be sandy, woosey, or rocky'.

And soon a stately line of houses and fine thoroughfares rose along the waterfront. Their names continue, reminding Dublin and Dubliners of a storied past. Where and when do Dubliners stumble on this storied past? Certainly the answer lies in chance encounters with old dockers and carters and seafarers who can describe with something more than pride the harsh poverty of their early lives. And certainly, in the still 'rememberable' past, it is in buying a drink for some old shawlie sitting alone in the snug, or 'biddy parlour', of a quayside tavern, quietly sipping and nursing her bottle of stout or ball o' malt as she:

> Peers at the rearward livin'
> And the years that have taken their toll,
> Just one of them darlin' ould-wans
> That have given our town its soul.

The purchased drink and the half-hour chat in such company is always time and money well spent. The entertainment value of such discourses is more frequently outweighed by the Aladdin's lamp discovery of some penetrating glimpse into the past.

Of course, the other great method of stumbling on some aspect of Dublin's history is through the purchase of second-hand books. A collection of old books and prints are always precious and attractive in themselves, but to the discerning eye and sensitive soul they transmit something of the pulse which gave life to the manners and the thinking of the past. Thirty, forty years ago Dublin had its picturesque book-barrow men selling their well-thumbed and dusty tomes from rickety stalls along the Liffeyside. Many a treasure I picked up there for a few pence. Alas, the barrow men are long since gone, but the spirit of the book barrows still hovers along the Liffey walls. The booksellers are still there in George Webb's and Robert's Bargain Books and Left Bank Books at Crampton Quay; the prints and old photographs at The Gallery of Photography, Wellington Quay; Professional Books at Ormond Quay; and just through the picturesque Merchant's Arch leading through Crown Alley into Temple Bar – not quite yet the Covent Garden of Dublin! – there's Halfpenny Bridge Books. A minute's stroll back across the bridge of the same name there's the quaintly named Winding Stairs Bookshop on Ormond Quay; here, any day of the week (and in a browser's paradise with windows overlooking the river) one can drink excellent coffee or soup while rubbing shoulders with many of Dublin's leading young poets, painters and writers.

I first stumbled on this magical world more than forty years ago. It was an old book barrow situated opposite the Corinthian cinema (now the Odeon) at Eden Quay and pitched up alongside a squat red-bricked building – was it a Corporation *pissoir* or some kind of gas or electrical sub-station? – and I remember the bookstall proprietor. He was a little man known simply as Joe. His bookshelves and benches were rude and rickety, designed for easy erection, easier dismantling and quick transportation from one pitch to the next by means of a sturdy handcart. Crude and makeshift, true, but the array of old books was a veritable kerbside university.

And one didn't frequent the old bookstalls solely for bargains. No; there was a unique camaraderie around the barrows, an egalitarianism that made a printer's devil, with no more than a shilling in his pocket, one with Trinity dons, doctors, bus conductors, civil servants, scholars and the raga-muffin *literati*. It was no foolish throng that I moved about in during those far-off days: old men, some shabbily dressed, others in the height of fashion, yet all fingering the volumes, poring over them, squinting, tilting, flicking, lingering – most of them reacquainting themselves with the companions of their youth and, most importantly for me, introducing those companions to an eager apprentice. Seeing the same old faces week after week I used to wonder sometimes if some of those old gentlemen had lost interest in the world's doings, or if they were without friends or family. I know better now.

The world of books is part and parcel of our perennial youth and our immortal souls. A good book can exempt us from from exhaustion and loneliness. The uncertainties of callow youth on the one hand and the corroding work of advanced years on the other are each deprived of half their sting in the companionship of books and of bookmen. We were students and apprentices and old men, rubbing shoulders with the displaced refugees of the pub's 'holy hour', with the drunks and the half-drunks and the dressed-up dandies and Teddy boys who had an hour to kill before a date with the 'mot' – a great, quiet democracy enriching our impoverished souls at the sixpenny barrows. I remember once getting a tap on the shoulder and a whispered aside which directed my attention to a small dark man in a raincoat hiccupping over a tattered book at the far end of the barrow. 'That's yo'r man Myles na gCopaleen', my informant nodded. And, God help my ignorance, I assumed at the time that Mr MacCopaleen was probably some Irish-speaking schoolmaster. On another occasion I remember elbowing past a rather portly, curly-headed fellow in an open-necked shirt – I think we engaged in a mumbled exchange of 'fuck off' – and later being informed that he was a house-painter named Behan who wrote plays in his spare time.

So there we were, almost every Saturday, above the low-tide stench of a summer's day or in the dreary spit-and-whip of winter wind that still had the salty tang of the sea in it before diesel fumes and double-deckers drove the beloved barrows away. There we were amongst the musty books, the very titles of which transferred us to other climes and times. Between shopping, cinema-queuing and the 'holy hour', we ran our fingers over tattered spines and riffled through dog-eared tomes and scanned the faded titles. Such simple exercises could elevate us to higher altitudes of thought!

An anonymous scribe of the last century once wrote: 'An inborn or an acquired taste for healthy literature is one of the choicest gifts of Providence, and should be coveted as one of Nature's most benificent endowments, as it furnishes the favoured individual with that intellectual recreation which calls forth the exercise of the noblest faculty which ranks him next to angels in the scale of creation.'

Angels by the Liffeyside? Hardly. Ah, but them was the days! It was at Joe's book barrow that I first came across a tattered and mildewed copy of that little gem *Ireland Sixty Years Ago* by John Edward Walsh (1816–69). Walsh, a barrister and later Attorney-General of Ireland and Master of the Rolls, published the book anonymously in the 1840s (though subsequent reprints were to carry his name). The initial anonymity is perhaps understandable in such an august upholder of the law desirous of maintaining 'propriety and decency, peace and good order'; but his book, nonetheless, is a colourful and graphic narrative of the underworld of Georgian Dublin, a lurid account of murders, abductions, faction fights, stabbings, duelling, gambling, highwaymen, hangings, gallows humour, prison slang and carousing – in short, a veritable litany of low life in eighteenth-century Dublin.

One suspects that despite Walsh's 'sober and wiser modes of thinking', the mature lawyer still had a sneaking regard for the hurly-burly riotousness of an era just vanishing when he was a boy. He was under no illusion that the age of Georgian splendour was necessarily an age of refinement; he knew that men and women of the highest fashion swore and drank like troopers, and that their excesses and violence contributed in no small measure to the darker traits of national life. It was an age of bull-baiting, cock-fighting and bareknuckle pugilism, when 'some ladies, at that time stars in the Irish court, were not very scrupulous in seeking such entertainment' and who frequently accosted street shoe-blacks for the delicious thrill of a coarse and ribald riposte, 'though they were not always fit to be repeated'. Walsh's own familiarity with prison slang and uncouth ballads – he gives copious footnotes to the 'unintelligible phrases' contained in the verses of 'Lord Altham's Bull', 'The Night Afore Larry Was Stretched', 'Luke Caffrey's Kilmainham Minit' and 'The May-Pole' – would indicate a knowledge and appreciation of colourful speech and coarse witticisms.

If all this seems a long digression from my pleasant saunter along the quays, then it is only by way of saying that it was in Walsh's book that I first learned of the bloody clashes along the same quays between the Liberty boys and their arch-rivals, the Ormond boys. Their long-standing and deadly feud was rooted in that accursed sectarianism which still, alas, so tragically bedevils a part of this island. The southside Liberty boys – mostly tailors, weavers and second-generation Huguenot petty tradesmen – were a strutting band of turbulent 'Protestants'; the northside Ormond boys – mainly butchers from the Ormond Market and their Smithfield cohorts – were an equally swaggering gang who flaunted their 'papist Catholicism' with a matching and extravagant defiance. Their battlefields were the bridges spanning the river that was intended to keep them apart.

Throughout most of the eighteenth century the bridges and quays of the Liffey became impassable, sometimes for days on end, as fierce battles raged between the weavers descending from Thomas Street and the butchers pouring out from the northside alleys. These were no mere skirmishes. The initial clashes for mastery of the bridges, bloody and hand-to-hand, were followed by 'lulls' of stone-throwing across the river until reinforcements arrived. On one occasion the Liberty boys were driven right back to their citadel of the Cornmarket and Thomas Street. Their stragglers were treated with the utmost ferocity – the temporarily victorious butchers indulged in an early form of knee-capping by using their long knives to 'hough' or slash through the leg tendons of their victims. When the Liberty boys rallied their forces for a counter-attack and then pursued their enemies all the way back to the Broadstone (a distance of nearly a mile), they wreaked vengeance on the Ormond stragglers by hanging them by their jaws from their own butchers' hooks in the market stalls. Walsh records: 'A friend of ours has told us, that he has gone down to Essex bridge, when he has been informed that one of those battles was raging, and stood quietly on the battlements for a whole day looking at the combat, in which above a thousand men were engaged.'

At such times, when the battles commencing on the quays extended as far upriver as Islandbridge, all shops were closed and business suspended. Lord Mayor Emerson declined to intervene, saying that it 'was as much as my life was worth to go among them'. The watchmen sent to apprehend the ringleaders were even more scared than the house-bound citizenry. They could only look on in terror. The soldiery from the Royal Barracks, once described as 'dangerous in times of peace and useless in times of war', were so raw-nerved on one occasion that when a musket accidentally clattered to the cobbles the whole squad wheeled round and fled back to quarters, strewing the quayside with sufficient pistols and bayonets to ensure a continuance of the fray for another few hours at least.

The smouldering times of the on-going feud were sometimes fanned into savage fire by such innocuous activities as the annual planting of the May Bush. (Finglas village, whose famous Maypole festivities still continued into the 1840s, was the chief resort of Dubliners on 1 May each year when Maypoles and May games were still popular.) Apparently, the Ormond boys cut down a bush in that vicinity annually, carried it back to Smithfield with one of their leaders astride it, and planted it in the centre of the square. On one occasion – recorded in Walsh's book and immortalised in the old ballad 'The May-Bush' – a 'commando' of the Liberty boys crossed the river and crept into the enemy camp at night, cut down the prized bush and sneaked away with their trophy. Bill Durham, alias Bill Dermot, a leader of the Ormond faction, pursued them with vows of revenge:

> For de loss of our bush, revenge we will get,
> Ri rigidi ri ri dum dee,
> In de slaughtering season we'll tip 'em a sweat,
> Rigidi di do dee,
> We'll wallop a mosey down Mead Street in tune,
> And we won't leave a weaver alive on de Coombe;

But we'll rip up his tripe-bag and burn his loom,
Ri rigidi di do dee!

Although a truce was signed between the Coombe and Smithfield contestants in 1748 and, no doubt to the great relief of the majority of the citizens, was prominently featured in the newspapers of the day, the peace seems to have been of that peculiarly Irish brand which is far more brittle and precarious than permanent. The bloody outbreaks continued to be reported up until 1790. Perhaps it took the threat of French invasion, or the brutalities attending on the Rising of 1798, to finally close the chapter on those barbarous, futile and petty re-enactments of the Boyne, Aughrim and Culloden?

Nor had Walsh any compunction in listing the number of his fellow jurists – eminent figures like Grattan, Lord Chancellor Fitzgibbon, O'Connell, Gifford, Philpot Curran (not to mention many lesser fry) – who, when they fell out on a point of law, or were bested in court, thought nothing of resuming the war of weighty words in a nearby field with swords or pistols. The practise and skill in the performance of the 'gentlemanly' code of duelling was almost a prerequisite for legal advancement. 'No gentleman had taken his proper station in life till he had "smelt powder", as it was called; no barrister could go circuit till he had obtained a reputation in this way; no election, and scarcely any assizes, passed without a number of duels; and many men of the bar, practising half a century ago, owed their eminence not to powers of eloquence or to legal ability, but to a daring spirit and the number of duels they had fought.'

Is there some significance in my catching the whiff of cordite and gunpowder just opposite the great drum and dome of the Four Courts?

James Gandon's magnificent eighteenth-century building (and his other masterpiece, the Custom House, which so splendidly counterbalances the Four Courts on the same river bank) have been so often and so well described by far better pens than mine that I think I am well advised to leave them alone. And perhaps both buildings would prefer it that way? For all their dignity and architectural finery, both the Four Courts and the Custom House comport themselves above the river with an air of surprise, and even wounded pride. Can you blame them? After more than a century of having their lineaments boasted, and looking down like *grand signeurs* on a townspeople who pointed them out to visitors as being among the chief adornments of the city, they suddenly found themselves being rounded upon by a section of the same townspeople and savagely attacked.

And poor Gandon – all his sumptuous interiors were either burned, bombed or blasted in the cause of Irish freedom! Fortunately, the shell-pocked and smoke-stained structures remained reasonably intact. The Custom House was one of the chief centres of British administration in Ireland until the Dublin Brigade of the old IRA set it alight in May 1921. A year later the Four Courts was seized by the anti-Treaty forces who used it for their headquarters during the uneasy peace that followed the evacuation of British troops from Ireland. Its shelling in June 1922 by pro-Treaty forces precipitated the Irish Civil War. The pro-Treaty shells were lobbed across the Liffey from the southside quays. It was the Liberty and Ormond boys all over again, though with more modern weapons and destructive accuracy. As in all such fratricidal strife, each side claimed the right and did so with the certitude that 'God is on our side' – an ironic reminder of that artillery parade of the Volunteers of the 1780s whose every cannon muzzle carried an ornate scroll bearing the splendid if somewhat sacrilegious phrase: 'Open thou our mouths, O Lord, and our lips shall show forth thy Praise.'

Enough said! And yet it seems to me that Gandon's masterpieces have never really gotten over the injury. Oh, they've uneasily accepted the apologies of expensive restoration ever since, but they have long memories. In 1967 that Hibernophile master of the short story, V. S. Pritchett, wrote: 'The quays of the Liffey do recall (but in a decaying mournful way) the quays of the Seine. The Dubliner likes to feel a bit French.' With respect, I don't think the Four Courts or the Custom House give a twopenny damn about being a bit French, despite the fact that Gandon was of Huguenot extraction. His buildings, or rather the ghosts who inhabit them, have other things on their minds. Since the 1960s the mournful decay along the quays has been deplorably rapid and extensive. Here and there – especially at Bachelor's Walk, where once fine houses have been gutted and their skeletons propped up with great and ugly baulks of timber – sites have been 'earmarked for an eyesore', in the words of one Dublin wag. To be fair, some attractive riverside replacements have recently appeared. And with them a few startling monstrosities have mushroomed along the same riverside! The ghosts within the Four Courts must surely turn away from the windows at night and shudder with disgust.

For ghosts there are. They stare down at the lamplight reflected in the unending and timeless ripples of water. They blink at the black shadows under the graceful arches of the old bridges. But they are puzzled and slightly apprehensive ghosts. They forgive – they've very little choice in the matter have they? – but they'll never forget. They are, come to think of it, in league with the cloth-capped and square-jawed docker further down the quays at Ringsend.

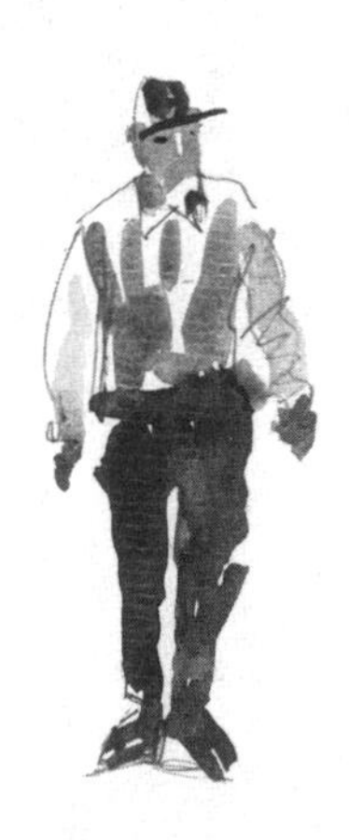

· 2 ·

Glasnevin

I NEVER hear Thomas Dunn English's delightful Victorian ballad 'Ben Bolt' without a certain quickening of the heart, especially the following verses:

> Don't you remember the schoolhouse, Ben Bolt
> With the master so cruel and so grim,
> And the shady nook by the babbling brook
> Where the children loved to swim.

It is a tender, lovely song and I am keenly sensitive to such evocations of nostalgia. In this instance I'm immediately transported back fifty years to a summer afternoon swimming in the Tolka River, just below the bridge in the shadow of the little wooden church of the Seven Dolours.

As an eight-year-old non-swimmer, it was my first-ever venture into 'out-of-depth' water. This was effected by the ingenious buoyancy aids invented by some of the older boys, a woolen scarf tied to the handles of a pair of tightly corked and disused two-gallon paraffin tins. The scarf was placed across the swimmer's chest and under the armpits so that the paraffin tins became floating 'water wings' in the region of the swimmer's shoulder blades. And they worked; it was a scarey, exhilarating experience to be fitted into the contraption and then towed out into the deep of shimmering water dappled by the tall, leafy trees overhanging 'the babbling brook'.

Another invention of those older Finglas boys was the use of their short-sleeved pullovers as makeshift swimming trunks – removing them, turning them upside down, placing their legs through the armholes so that the neck aperture now dangled about their knees, and then securing the waist hem of the garment about their midriffs by means of a belt or a piece of twine. Often enough, the weight of the drooping, sodden wool at the 'trock' pulled the garment out from under the belt, with the usual predictable guffaws and jeers.

And in the late afternoon, with the first whisper of breeze through the leaves, and awash with laughter, splashings, duckings and the bravery of our essay into the deep, we pulled on our clothes, wrung out the soggy pullovers, gathered up the magical paraffin drums and pooled our ha'pennies for a homeward feast of bulls eyes and honeybee bars.

Somewhere above us, from the open door of the pub at the bridge (now called the Tolka House), a bar-room tenor, unashamedly sentimental despite the coarse timbre of his voice, was filling the evening with his song:

> In the old churchyard in the village, Ben Bolt
> In a corner obscure and alone
> They've fitted a slab of the granite so grey
> And Alice lies under the stone.

The old churchyard of Glasnevin stands at the top of the Cinderpath Lane connecting Mobhi Road and Ballymun Road – the 'real' Glasnevin cemetery, according to some of the older local people. What Dubliners refer to as Glasnevin cemetery is more correctly termed 'Prospect cemetery' and was founded by Daniel O'Connell in 1832. The watch-towers on the wall of this larger and better-known graveyard are standing testimony to that era of bodysnatchers, grave robbers, 'resurrectionists' and 'sack-em-up' men. It was a time when the legal and public dissection of hanged criminals under the surgeon's knife did not, apparently, provide sufficient specimens for the advancement of medical science. There was a brisk trade in the looting of fresh graves and the trundling of macabre bundles through the night. A notable medical man and city coroner of the day, Dr Kirwan, was pinned against a tomb one night by a brace of bloodhounds. He tried to fight them off with his walking stick. His cries, and the noise of the snarling dogs, quickly brought the night watchmen and dog-handlers to his assistance. The doctor claimed that he was merely taking a shortcut through the deserted graveyard when set upon by the hounds. But was he there for some other purpose?

I cannot think what lured my mind into such gloomy thoughts unless it was, as a consequence of a recent visit to the cemetery, the sight of so many pale crosses and tombstones in the evening mist; the Victorian monuments and the ivy-covered trees lead me to consider how strange it all seems that there's only a wall between the people's tombs and the people's pleasure-ground – for Prospect cemetery and the Botanic Gardens lie cheek-by-jowl. Both are synonymous with Glasnevin. The 168.5-foot O'Connell memorial round tower in the graveyard and the curvilinear range of glasshouses in the Botanic Gardens evoke the district no less surely than Delville and the letters of Mrs Delaney.

There is a legend which tells how St Berchan (better known as Moibhi Clairaineach, 'the cripple') blessed for all time the Tolka River and the land around Glasnevin. Fourteen hundred years have passed since then and many changes have come to the locality. For centuries the land around was farmed extensively by the monks of the Priory of All Hallows, but after the Reformation the land was leased out to some of the great Anglo-Irish families, such as the Bathes and Ushers. In the sixteenth century Glasnevin was described as a small village with a church, a bull ring, a tailor, a shoemaker and a few farm hands. By 1664 the number of inhabitants was only ten, the houses being rated for one chimney each. The most prominent residence was 'a good stone house with out-offices and a garden and orchard' known as the Glen. Later, through the writings of Swift and the correspondence of Mrs Delaney, this house was to acquire enduring fame as Delville.

Delville was leased in 1719 to two fellows of Trinity College, Dr Helsham and Dr Delaney, who christened it Heldelville. Delaney (Rector of St Werburgh's) soon after acquired sole possession and plumped for the more prudent title of Delville, though the name change is usually attributed to his friend Dean Swift:

> But you, forsooth your all must squander
> On that poor spot called Dell-ville yonder,

> And when you've been at base expenses
> In whims, parterres, canals and fences,
> Your assets fail and cash is wanting
> Nor further buildings, further planting . . .

Swift thus satirised the folly and extravagance of Delaney, who hoped that by a combination of sumptuous hospitality and blatant flattery he might attain advancement in the Church. Of humble stock, Delaney yearned for wealth, influence and position. And, with a healthy opinion of his own talents, he believed himself at least worthy of a bishopric, and that this was the best way of going about it. He may not have been too far wrong. 'Few – and very few – are the adducible instances in which, in the reigns of George III, George IV, and William IV, a bishop was appointed for evangelistic zeal or pastoral efficiency; But, on whatever principal chosen, the bishop, once duly consecrated and enthroned, was a formidable person, and surrounded by a dignity scarcely less than royal' (G. W. E. Russell, *Collections and Recollections*, London: Nelson & Sons, 1903).

First Delaney levelled the old Glen house, designed a new villa-type residence and had gardens laid out in the latest Dutch fashion. 'The rurality of it is wonderfully pretty', Mrs Delaney later wrote, going on to describe how it was planted 'in a *wild way* . . . you would not imagine it the work of art'. The work of art almost wrecked Delaney financially. He therefore cast about for a wealthy widow and quickly found one in Margaret Tenison of County Louth. Back in business, so to speak, and with comparative opulence, he was soon able to entertain more lavishly. Lord Carteret, the Lord-Lieutenant, was invited to Delville and secured for Delaney a living in County Fermanagh and chancellorship of Christ Church. A 'living' in those days didn't mean an uprooting from Delville, merely the receipt of most of the tithes and revenues of the parish in far-off Fermanagh while a deputy performed all the religious duties! Nice work if you can get it, and the Reverend Delaney (detained in Dublin by business and pleasure) was getting it. The transitions of prebendary, dean, prelate, and 'the long train of purple, profit, and power' were on the move.

Then, in 1741, Margaret died and Delaney was soon involved in litigation with her daughter from her previous marriage, legal quarrelling that was to vex him right up until his death twenty-seven years later. Meanwhile, however, a second rich widow had to be urgently found, preferably one with aristocratic connections and political contacts who might use her influence to obtain the elusive bishopric. Time was running out for the fifty-eight-year-old clergyman. He hurried to London, found what he was looking for in the forty-four-year-old Mary Granville, rapidly wooed her and quietly married her in June 1743.

This second Mrs Delaney – *the* Mrs Delaney – fell in love with Delville, and, as an accomplished letter-writer, we are indebted to her for so much information about Glasnevin and Dublin in the eighteenth century. She gives us fine descriptions of the house and its furnishings and records with evident pride the number of servants, and her dinners and receptions for a new crop of influential guests: Lord and Lady Chesterfield (he was the viceroy who did so much to improve Phoenix Park), Primate Stone and his sister, the Bishop of Derry and his wife, and so on. The luxury of the period was prodigal rather than refined, and at Delville the splendours of domestic living, as depicted in Mrs Delaney's letters, reveal a dinner for four consisting of: 'Fish-beefstakes – soups – rabbit and onions – Fillet Veal – Turkey pout – salmon grilde – pickled salmon – quails – little Terrene Peas – Cream – Mushrooms – Apple Pye – Crab – Leveret – Cheese-cakes – Blamange – Cherries – Dutch Cheese – Raspberries and Cream – sweetmeats and jelly – strawberries and cream – almond cream – currants and gooseberries – Orange Butter'. In a letter from Delville dated October 1764, a menu for the Delaneys and ten guests details: 'Turbot and Soles, remove Ham; Force meat etc.; two partridges and two grouse; rabbits and onions; Pies; sweetbreads and crumbs; Salmigundi; Soup; Boiled chicken; Collop veal and olives; pease; Cream Pudding; Plumb Crocant; Chine of Mutton; Turkey in jelly; Hare; Lobster Fricassee'. The items are not divided into courses, but there is a note under 'Dessert': 'Nine things – six of them fruit out of our own garden, and a plate of fine Alpine Strawberries'.

Despite Mrs Delaney's undoubted charm and her gastronomical exertions on the heroic scale, however, the coveted bishopric for her spouse remained unrealised. And all was not sunshine and pleasure among this talented group of clergymen by the Tolka. Swift, a constant visitor (and who in all probability printed some of his most dangerous pamphlets in a cellar at Delville), was first to feel the disappointment of thwarted ambition. Hoping to be offered a bishopric by Queen Anne for his service to the Tory cause, he could do no more than extort from her ministers the Deanery of St Patrick's in Dublin – an ecclesiastical dignity of no great value to him and requiring residence in a country he despised, no matter how much he loved and served its hapless citizens. Added to that were the complex and tangled romances with Stella and Vanessa and, cruellest blow of all, the tragedy of their untimely deaths. By this time also there were ominous signs that the curse of madness was about to afflict him. The terrible fits of dizziness and deafness which had assailed him from early manhood were about to destroy his once great mind – 'the fatal rocks towards which his logic desperately drifted', as Thackeray puts it. And Scott recounts a story of how Delaney once happened on Swift and Archbishop King in earnest conversation. It was a conversation which left the prelate in tears, and from which he hurried away with 'marks of strong terror and agitation in his countenance'. Archbishop King then turned to Delaney and tearfully said, 'You have just met the most unhappy man on earth; but on the subject of his wretchedness you must never ask a question.'

Poor Delaney scarcely fared better. Though elevated to the Deanery of Down he still wasn't satisfied. In his mid sixties he was suddenly compelled to exercise economies at Delville due to an adverse decision in a law suit. The dream of enthronement was fading fast. He wrote a posthumous defence of his friend Swift – even though the latter had once said that all Delaney's writings were best left unread! – and, almost impoverished, died in May 1768 aged eighty-three. He was buried in a part of the garden of Delville which was later added to the Protestant churchyard mentioned earlier, and is now chiefly remembered for the fact that he was the second Mrs Delaney's husband and the friend of Swift. Anne

Granville Pendarves Delaney survived him by twenty years and retired to England. Her letters and the genius of Swift add lustre to Glasnevin and ensure that while Delville is no more (the Bon Secours Hospital now occupies the site), it shall always be remembered and associated with he whom Thackeray described as 'Dean Drapier Bickerstaff Gulliver – the most famous statesmen and the greatest poets of his day had applauded him and done him homage. And at this time all the great wits of England had been at his feet. All Ireland had shouted after him, and worshipped him as liberator, a saviour, the greatest Irish patriot and citizen.'

There is a theory, or maybe just another one of those Dublin rumours, to the effect that Swift's tragic demise in the insane hospital which he had founded out of his large-hearted charity created a resistance among the Lilliputians to his being actually interred within the precincts of St Patrick's Cathedral. His memorial and epitaph ('where savage indignation can no longer lacerate his heart') in the cathedral's west-end nave lie close to that of his beloved Stella and are in the form of a wall tablet sculpture which, as a general rule in old churches, signifies that there may be a coffin or an urn of ashes underneath. However, if it is a cenotaph – that is, a memorial to someone buried elsewhere – then it might support the theory that his grave lies somewhere else. This theory, or rumour, further maintains that the Reverend Dr Delaney had Swift's remains privately buried at Delville, perhaps in that same plot which was later to be incorporated in the old churchyard.

The instincts of a mystery writer inclines me to the view that there is substance in the tale. And the instincts of a historical romanticist reinforce the view if only for the fact that – in spite of what may appear to be (and what scant history suggests to be) the shallowness of Delaney's life and the tawdriness of his ambitions – this one gesture alone deserves that he too should be remembered in his own worth.

The other great houses beside the Tolka in those days were 'Teeling's Tenement' and Glasnevin House. The former was situated in what is now the Botanic Gardens and the latter was just a little to the north of it on high ground overlooking the Tolka. One became the home of the poet

Thomas Tickell, the other the home of Sir John Rogerson, ship-owner, enterprising businessman, member of parliament, Lord Mayor, and a man who gave his name to one of the Liffey quays. Tickell, a political appointee of Addison's, was secretary to the Lord Justices of Ireland and held this office while residing at Glasnevin, until his death in 1740. Rogerson wisely invested in land and acquired extensive estates in Fermanagh (the earls of Erne were descended from him in the female line). He came to Glasnevin when the tiny village, according to Archbishop King's account, had a reputation for dishonesty and immorality; Tickell came to it some years later, about the time it was being made respectable by Swift and Delaney and when it was earning the reputation of an idyll for clergymen poets like Thomas Parnell (1679–1718), Vicar of Finglas and Archdeacon of Clogher, and the playwright Thomas Southerne. Born just 'down the road' at Oxmantown Green in 1659 – where the town's well-to-do loved to play bowls at the time – Southerne's dramas were considered among the best of their age. He gave the English language such phrases as: 'I think, therefore I am' and 'Do pity me. Pity's akin to love', the latter from his drama *Oroonoko* (1696), which the eminent Victorian critic Henry Hallam notes as the very first English work to denounce the slave trade of the seventeenth and later centuries and to condemn the horrors of enforced transportation to the West Indies.

Tickell's 'Ode on the Death of Addison', containing the lines:

> He taught us how to live;
> And (Oh! Too high the price for knowledge)
> taught us how to die

was judged by both Goldsmith and Johnson to be 'one of the finest in the language'. Similarly, his ballad 'Colin and Lucy' was reckoned by the good-humoured John Gay to be 'the best and prettiest in the world':

> I hear a voice you cannot hear,
> Which says I must not stay;

I see a hand you cannot see,
Which beckons me away.

Teeling's Tenement, or if like me you prefer Tickell's Grove, was sold by the poet's family for £2,000 to Dr Wade in order to establish a botanic garden. The Botanic Gardens – unlike some of the nefarious and nocturnal activities once associated with the adjoining Prospect cemetery – was especially bought and cultivated on behalf of the Dublin medical profession who had always recognised and appreciated the curative properties of many herbs and plants.

> Without a botanical garden, how can the apothecary know the plants he employs in his shop and compositions, how can the physician know the plants he prescribed or examine the nature or virtue of them, or the cook or confectioner avoid those of deliterious nature . . . the greenhouse should have brought us acquaintance with medicines of very extraordinary virtues hitherto but little known, and time may bring to our knowledge many more of these if there was but proper places to raise them . . . is not the beauty of the flower garden of some account? . . . I could add many other reasons for encouraging good public gardens, and finding a proper curator for them . . .

So wrote Dr Patrick Browne of Mayo in 1788. Opened in March 1795, the Botanic Gardens owe their existence to such writings and to the efforts of the botanist Wade, the philanthropic merchant Pleasants and the Speaker of the Irish House of Commons, John Foster. Wade, 'tricked out in apparel as tawdry as the pie-bald vestiture of the high priest of Flora herself', was motivated by a life-long love of botany, Pleasants by a desire to further adorn Georgian Dublin with a fine public recreational park, and Foster by the dual aims of promoting Irish agriculture and hence landlordly profits. Their combined efforts and motivations produced an admirable result.

The garden had predecessors of sorts: a campus kitchen garden for the scholars and fellows of Trinity College in the 1680s; a 'fair garden for plants' at Crow Street (Temple Bar) under the auspices of Molyneaux and Petty's Dublin

Philosophical Society in the 1690s; a further botanical garden at Ballybough Bridge (now the Luke Kelly Bridge) in 1732 and, three years later, at Great Martin's Lane (now Railway Street). In 1687 the provost and fellows of Trinity College agreed to convert their kitchen garden of 'cabbages, artichokes and a host of different salads' into a physic garden. The physic garden, abandoned about 1773, doesn't appear to have been a great success or a very salubrious place; located behind the Anatomy Theatre it was inhabited by thousands of rats scavenging among the offal discarded from the dissecting rooms!

After Delville and Tickell's Grove the other great residence was, of course, Rogerson's Glasnevin House. His family later sold it on to Henry Mitchell MP, a wealthy banker with a genuine skill and love of horticulture. His gardens – predating the adjoining Botanic Gardens and, perhaps, inspiring their location? – were justly famous and greatly admired in their time. After Mitchell's death Glasnevin House passed through many hands until it eventually came into the possession of Charles Lindsay, Bishop of Kildare and Dean of Christ Church. Ah, a bishop at last!

It would be nice to think that Lindsay, like those other Anglican divines – Swift, Parnell, Delaney et al – jostling and angling for preferment along the banks of the Tolka, had finally attained a coveted bishopric. But this was not the case. Lindsay was neither a native, a poet, nor of humble 'scribbling' stock. He was a scion of one of the great Scottish families, son of the Earl of Crawford and Balcarres – the family were proprietors in the Glasnevin district, leasing land at seven pounds per acre at a time when the best-paid labouring men could earn nine shillings per week – and the present-day Lindsay and Crawford roads commemorate the connection. But, oh, how the Delaneys would have loved to entertain him!

Before old Bishop Lindsay died in 1846, the historian D'Alton listed the population of Glasnevin at 964 persons and tells of quarries of blackstone on the banks of the Tolka and a weaving factory with a dozen looms which produced sailcloth and canvas. D'Alton's visit in 1834 also mentions a Protestant school with thirty-five pupils founded by Bishop

Lindsay, though this perhaps may be confused with the famous 'Ink-bottle' school – which, according to tradition, was founded by Swift a century before, and who suggested its peculiar, circular and 'ink-bottle' shape. Opposite the school was an almshouse founded in 1723 which gave shelter and a shilling and eightpence a week to four poor widows – is the date another indication of Swiftian influence and concern? The 'Ink-bottle' was demolished in the early years of this century, and some time after his death Bishop Lindsay's residence became the present convent of the Sisters of the Holy Faith.

The stretch of river running between the convent on the high ground and the Botanic Gardens below has always been one of my favourite places. We – that is, my wife and I – visit it as often as possible and together have been coming here for nigh on forty years (and in Mary's case much longer, for as a child, in the 1940s, she was a day pupil at the Holy Faith). It is still one of the most delightful places by the side of a once-beautiful river, now increasingly sullied by suburbia.

The Tolka rises in County Meath near Batterstown, and hence about twenty miles from its exit to the sea at East Wall. There is a kind of rough music – like water gurgling over old stones – in the names of the townlands through which it passes: Fairyhouse, Dunboyne, Clonee, Mulhuddart, Blanchardstown, Dunsinea, Ashtown, Scribblestown, Cardiff's Bridge, Finglas, Glasnevin, Drumcondra, Clonliffe, Ballybough, East Wall. For all I know, it may still be quite beautiful near its source and upper reaches, but it is frequently less so as it tries to hurry through the ever-spreading suburbs with their discarded beer cans and the dismal banners of plastic bags hanging limply from bankside twigs. Still, all is not lost. In my ramblings of late I've found signs of renewal, and certainly the Parks Department of Dublin Corporation are to be commended for their excellent work at Tolka River Park and Griffith Park. Similar renewal is to be found at East Wall, where the local amateur canoeists have made a dam of stones to form a 'training' pool and, beside it, have painstakingly scooped out a tiny channel giving access to the open sea at times of low tide – a practical and inventive feat on a par with the paraffin-drum water wings of long ago. Bravo!

Often, by this favourite stretch of the Tolka, we have mused and wondered about that flowering of poetic activity along its banks for a few decades in the early eighteenth century. Was this fortuity, propinquity and the natural outcome of a happy interchange of thought among talented and like-minded people? 'Great souls by instinct to each other turn/Demand alliance, and in friendship burn', wrote Addison (who is said to have frequently visited his friend Tickell at Glasnevin). Or had something of St Mobhi's blessing seeped down through history, linking the monkish scriveners of the past with these latter poets and priests?

The place abounds in such associations. It is an idyll for daydreamers. It was here, picnicking by the stream in our courtship days, that Mary first told me about Bishop Lindsay and how his sister, Lady Anne Barnard, wrote the popular Scottish ballad 'Auld Robin Grey.' In 1771 young Anne, enthralled by an ancient traditional Scots air sung to her by an old family retainer – though, as befitted a bishop's sister (and one who was later to wed the son of a bishop of Limerick) she deprecated the use of so many 'improper' words in the old ballad – decided to modernise the song. 'I longed to sing old Sophy's air to different words, and give to its plaintive tones some little history of virtuous distress in humble life, such as might suit it', she explained to Sir Walter Scott in a letter many years later. Her anonymous verses, allied to the old melody, became an immediate success, one of the earliest instances of a hit tune. A reward of twenty guineas – thousands, by the money of our day – was offered in the newspapers for the author's identity.

And it was here too – perhaps on the very same day as our picnic? – that my beloved daydreamer diffidently showed me the first schoolgirl poem she'd ever written:

> I sit like a bump on a log by the stream,
> Ears filled with bird-song, soul bathed in green,
> Lindsay ghosts ripple the Tolka's brown flow,
> Pale rhododendrons, fragile pink glow.
> Pythagoras Theoram open on lap,

Nothing between my two ears but a gap!
Leaves shadow-dancing on sun-dappled pond,
Disapprobation from red school beyond!

There is, and always has been, a kind of magic about the Tolka at Tickell's Grove and Glasnevin.

· 3 ·

O'Connell Street & Grafton Street

DUBLIN is a capital city and it looks the part; it didn't require the establishment of an independent Free State to be assured of its 'capital-ness'. Ever since Olaf was crowned first Norse king of Dublin in 853 – perhaps ever since Ptolemy's Eblana? – the town was quietly grooming itself for the role. In time it was to become the second city of an empire and to have its own vice-regal court. You feel that perhaps coronets, tiaras and ermine-trimmed cloaks might still be found in the attics and cellars of some its Georgian houses.

And ever since the 1750s when Luke Gardiner pulled down all the old houses in Drogheda Street (widening it greatly on the west side so that a span of 150 feet separated the rows of new houses), then laid out a tree-lined walk down the middle of what quickly became known as Gardiner's Mall (later Sackville Street and now O'Connell Street), this handsome thoroughfare has been the high street of a nation. Two hundred and fifty years of elegance, tawdriness, traffic, history, processions, commerce, demonstrations, riot and gunfire have marched, wheeled, jostled, clamoured, hawked and reverberated along its length. At one time it was considered to be among the finest streets in Europe. Over a seven-year stretch a rebellion and a civil war reduced it to rubble. The sole surviving Georgian Mansion (Lord Gosford's, number 42) was until sometime in the 1960s the Catholic Commercial Club, the upstairs interior of which is now incorporated with pleasing effect as a restaurant in the Royal Dublin Hotel. Out of the Troubles grew a street containing some of the worst features of 1920s taste, a fact which probably assisted its downward slide to the ice-cream parlour and cinema strip so beloved of us as children. In the 1940s there were six picture houses, as I recall: the Grand Central, the Astor, the

Metropole, the Pillar, the Carleton and the Savoy. Only the last two remain. And today, even though O'Connell Street seems to have more or less thrown in the towel in its struggle against the ravages of hamburger bars, juke boxes, slot machines and fast-food joints, it is still, nonetheless, a vibrant, often dramatic, streetscape.

Indeed, if I had to recommend an activity to a first-time visitor with only a few hours at his or her disposal, and who was keen to learn something of the spirit and story of Dublin, then I would unhesitatingly suggest a morning stroll, preferably a spring morning when the exhilarating air has the zing of champagne in it and the faces of passers-by are aglow with instant pleasing. Begin the stroll from the north end of O'Connell Street, traversing its length, cross over the bridge, through Westmoreland Street, passing the College and the Bank (the still intimate quality of this capital city ensures that everyone knows this to mean Trinity College and the Bank of Ireland), and proceed leisurely up Grafton Street and on to the entrance of St Stephen's Green. All Dublin life is here. The statues and monuments on the way tell their own tales. It is the route and the domain of buskers, balladeers, beggars and 'chalkies' (those pavement artists who, literally down on their hands and knees to earn a crust and indifferent to posterity, daub our pavements and enrich our lives with their multi-coloured masterpieces). If all Dublin streets are a stage echoing great events, contradictions and buffoonery, then the route just described is an opera house. There is a novel, or at least a short story, in any one of its statues and monuments, not excepting its most celebrated and imposing one which 'disappeared' overnight, as it were, a quarter of a century ago.

Nelson's Pillar, or Column, was the city's most conspicuous and best-known landmark for 157 years; it was the terminus for the trams, the meeting-place for lovers, the hub on which the daily lives of the citizens revolved, the centre of our universe. 'I'll meet you at the Pillar' was our slogan; all tram scrolls and destination boards carried the legend: 'To Nelson's Pillar' or just simply 'the Pillar' before the great turnabout at the base of the monument meant a scattering to Dalkey, Dollymount, Rathmines or Whitehall. *An Lar* contains no such poetry.

Built in 1808–1809 to a height of 134 feet and surmounted by a statue of Admiral Nelson by Thomas Kirk, it was commissioned just after the battle of Trafalgar by a grateful committee of Dublin merchants, ship-owners and bankers who rejoiced in a naval victory that meant a re-opening of sea-lanes to mercantile shipping. Though shorter than its London counterpart, 'our Nelson' had the greater advantage of a spiral staircase within which, for a few pence, one could climb dizzily to the top and even more dizzily overlook the GPO, O'Connell Street, much of the city and the mountains beyond. It was said that no true 'Dublinman' (as distinct from a 'Dubliner', who is merely a resident and lacking in the mandatory three or four generations 'on the Ma and the Da's side') would ever climb to the top of the Pillar. Such a worthless exercise was only for tourists, culshies and blow-ins, but such niceties of pedigree and definition never deterred us as youngsters from making the ascent.

Nor was the average Dublinman or Dubliner – unlike some of the more sensitive and petty-minded patriots – unduly concerned by the fact that it was a monument to a British hero, an imperialist and an anachronistic symbol. Like that other great Napoleonic memorial, the Wellington Testimonial obelisk in Phoenix Park, its phallic connotations caused more ribald comment than indignation. 'Yo'r Nelson' was once a sobriquet for the male sexual organ. Perhaps for this reason alone it was as well that nothing ever came of the many suggestions since the foundation of the state to the effect that Nelson's statue be taken down and replaced with either St Patrick, John Kennedy, the Pope, the Sacred Heart or the Blessed Virgin. The affectionate ribaldry was too deeply entrenched.

Still, there was always a considerable body of opinion anxious to have the 'big yoke' pulled down completely. Ultra-nationalists often attacked it on the grounds that it was a political anomaly; others used the pretence that it was an obstruction to traffic; some felt it should be re-erected at one end or other of the thoroughfare instead of in the middle where it visually reduced the length of the street. Yeats, while agreeing that it should be retained if only because 'the life and work of the people who erected it is a part of our tradition', didn't consider it beautiful. Maurice Craig did: 'I think it both beautiful and well-placed, for it helps, with the G.P.O., to redeem O'Connell Street, potentially so beautiful, from a squalid disorder almost equal to parts of London.' The matter was decided once and for all by that arbitrary cabal which permits of no debate: the extremist bombers. In 1966, on the eve of the Golden Jubilee commemorations of the 1916 Rising, they blasted the monument to smithereens. Miraculously, no one was injured that night. Like so many of us, V. S. Pritchett lamented its destruction: 'it gave O'Connell Street a dignity which now has almost gone. It marked the centre of Dublin, gave it gaiety.'

To Yeats is attributed that Dublin saying – the pungency of which is reduced by a third through the loss of the aforesaid monument – claiming that the capital of holy Ireland is notable for having the statues of three adulterers in its main street: Parnell, Nelson and O'Connell. Yeats further outraged Irish Catholic opinion when, speaking during the Senate debate on divorce legislation in June 1925, he remarked that: 'It was said about O'Connell in his own day, that you could not throw a stick over a workhouse wall without hitting one of his children', a reference to the *Times* charging the Liberator with the parentage of broods of illegitimate children in Dublin and Kerry. The charge, and the rumours, were fuelled by the publication in 1832 of a pamphlet entitled *A Narrative by Miss Ellen Courtenay of most extraordinary Cruelty, Perfidy and Depravity perpetrated against her by Daniel O'Connell, Esq. (M.P. for Kerry)*. But as Miss Courtenay's tale of seduction and betrayal contained almost as much text denouncing O'Connell's politics, and, in a letter written to O'Connell's parliamentary colleague O'Gorman Mahon in the year before publication of the pamphlet (and obviously with the intention of letting O'Connell know her design), she states that she had been 'strongly urged by many persons . . . to publish the facts – it would make her fortune', the whole thing may have been a scheme of blackmail.

Parnell's Monument is another reminder of the *Times* and

its attacks on an Irish leader. The story of the Pigott forgeries and the O'Shea Divorce Case are perhaps too well known to merit inclusion here in any detail. The wretched Pigott – a venal and meanly ambitious hack journalist – tried to give himself a lift up in life by selling a collection of letters to the *Times* purporting to be in Parnell's handwriting and linking him to complicity in crime, specifically the Phoenix Park murders. Not only Parnell, who vehemently denounced the letters as 'villainous and bare-faced' forgeries, but the entire Irish nationalist movement was on trial. Under relentless cross-examination Pigott broke down and confessed to forgery. Ruined and discredited he fled to Madrid and blew his brains out in a shabby hotel room. Vindicated, Parnell received standing ovations everywhere as the 'uncrowned King of Ireland'.

But not for long. Alas, he did not emerge so well from the aftermath of the case in which that Captain O'Shea (who seemed determined to betray everyone at least once) brought divorce proceedings against his wife Kitty. Parnell, cited for adultery, did not answer the charge. His affair with Mrs O'Shea is a touching story of deep and passionate love, as true and pathetic as it is tragic. It was for the lovers and for Ireland. The divorce, and Parnell's subsequent marriage to Kitty O'Shea, precipitated the Chief's downfall and created a split in Catholic Ireland that launched a bitter feud which was only replaced by the enmities of the Civil War thirty years later. The prime mover in the split was Parnell's erstwhile lieutenant Tim Healy, a man far superior to O'Shea in matters of betrayal, and one who did so with a venom and viciousness that allowed him to boast that he would drive Parnell into the grave or into an insane asylum. Having assisted hugely in achieving the first aim – for poor Parnell was dead within a year – Healy's 'poisoned tongue' excoriated the victim's widow as 'that British prostitute'. Breandan O hEithir in his excellent book *The Begrudger's Guide to Irish Politics* quotes St John Ervine's description of Healy as having 'a sort of purity which became nauseous because it was unaccompanied by any kind of charity. This bitter tongue leapt out of his mouth when he spoke of anyone who had fallen into mortal sin; and when he referred to a woman who had offended against the law, he did so in terms that made even the strong of stomach feel sick.' This same Tim Healy (suspected by some to be that mysterious and shadowy double agent 'Thorpe', the longest-serving and most important of Dublin Castle's spies and informers at the time) later became, and ended his days, as the first Governor-General of the Irish Free State!

When people put up a statue to a man, they leave it to posterity and guide books to save him from oblivion. But in Dublin only the statues of the winning side survive. The effigies of the losing team – Nelson, the plump Victoria that sat outside Leinster House until 1949, King Billy astride his charger in College Green until 1929, Field-Marshal Lord Gough similarly mounted in Phoenix Park until 1956, Viceroy Eglinton at St Stephen's Green – all were unceremoniously blasted or carted away to oblivion. Even that gentle poet and essayist Tom Kettle of Malahide was discommoded by a temporary 'beheading' for no greater crime than having been killed in France while serving with the Dublin Fusiliers in the First World War:

> Know that we fools, now with the foolish dead,
> Died not for flag, nor King, nor Emperor –
> But for a dream, born in a herdsman's shed,
> And for the secret Scripture of the poor.

But a statue's survival doesn't necessarily exempt it from irreverent comment or a 'bit of divilment'. For a season or two when I was growing up it was a practise of some late-night revellers and hardchaws to climb onto the Parnell statue and place an empty beer bottle on Parnell's outstretched hand. The irony of the outstretched hand pointing in the direction of the Rotunda maternity hospital and allied to Parnell's oft-quoted, and misquoted, words emblazoned on the monument above his head: 'No man has a right to fix the boundary to the march of a nation' was not lost on Dublin wags of the past. The fact, too, that the sculptor August St Gaudens appears to have dressed Parnell in two overcoats suggested to the same wags that 'the poor man needs them, standin' at a draughty crossroads day and night' and that the outer coat was probably intended as a protection against bird droppings:

> Parnell's statue starts the street, though pigeon shit doth mottle
> The outstretched arm that often times may hold an empty bottle.
> (No man can put a boundary mark to the marching of a nation
> Much less curb the midnight drunk in the midst of his elation!)

The other monuments lining the centre of the street – memorials to temperance crusader Father Mathew, Labour leader Jim Larkin, politician and newspaper baron Sir John Gray, patriot and revolutionary William Smith O'Brien, the O'Connell Monument and the Anna Livia Fountain – are generally treated with more civility. No, on reflection I must exclude Anna Livia! All are periodically clambered upon, clung to, precariously embraced and pressed into service by the more agile young citizens as vantage points to view such processions as the annual St Patrick's Day parade, when, as one such enthusiastic spectator called out: 'Sure isn't it great to see the Irish shamrock marchin' arm-in-arm with the Statue of Liberty?' The newest of these sculptures, Anna Livia (an elongated female figure reclining in a fountain and representing the Liffey) dates from the city's millennial celebrations in 1988 and was presented by the well-known businessman Michael Smurfit. It was no sooner unveiled when the lads christened it 'the Floozie in the Jacuzzi', though it is also referred to as the 'whore in the sewer' and 'Bidet Mulligan', once again showing the Dubliner's instinct for affectionate raillery and the apposite nickname.

I remember once, about twenty-five years ago, slowly walking around the O'Connell Monument and noting the bullet holes in the arms and breasts of the quartet of buxom angels, or winged victories, seated at the base. They were tiny but grim reminders of the Troubles fifty years before. On my second orbit of John Henry Foley's fine sculptures an old-timer, sunning himself on one of the seats, suddenly closed his newspaper and, raising the mild challenge of his blue eyes to follow my gaze, muttered: 'D'Esterre's revenge, what?'

'I beg your pardon?'

'D'Esterre's revenge. The bullet holes. Maybe they were meant for O'Connell, not the angels. D'you ever think of that?' He was ready to launch into narrative. I was ready to listen.

I have mentioned elsewhere how duelling was considered to be the hallmark of a gentleman lawyer 200 years ago. O'Connell was no exception in this regard. He once quarrelled with a political rival, Captain John Neville D'Esterre, a member of Dublin Corporation, and in the resulting duel D'Esterre was killed. He was the one fatal victim of O'Connell's duelling days. And it was O'Connell's last duel. He was frequently 'called out' in after life, often with taunts and extreme provocation, but such was his remorse at having killed D'Esterre that he turned away from the challenges. It was an age when such refusals were thought cowardice; the future champion of Moral Force, with a growing horror of bloodshed, showed more courage by his steadfast determination never to take up the gauntlet again. At the time he tried to make amends by offering to 'share his income' and settle a handsome annuity on D'Esterre's widow. She declined; but some years later, when O'Connell was snowed under with important and lucrative briefs in Dublin, he somehow learned that the woman was in great difficulties through involvement in a major law suit in Cork. He immediately threw up all his business and travelled post haste down to Cork to plead her case and win it. He later settled an annuity on D'Esterre's daughter which was faithfully paid until death. A regular Mass-goer and frequent communicant, O'Connell never afterwards approached the alter rail without wearing a black glove on his 'duelling' right hand to remind him of his unworthiness.

'And never,' said my informant, 'never after did Dan pass by D'Esterre's house – just up the quay there, 11 Bachelor's Walk, so it is – without respectably raisin' his hat and sayin' a prayer for the soul of poor D'Esterre and for the poor family within.' My narrator of twenty-five years ago was one of that vanishing breed who make the town a more agreeable place for all who happen to meet up with them. They exult in old tales. They love to recount and share them. There is no guile. Whatever is in their minds is available on the instant. Chance encounter with members of the breed are reminders of Lamb's definition of happiness: contentment with the condition of being 'no wiser, no richer, and no handsomer' than one's neighbour. And with his tale told the narrator deftly creased his newspaper back into its original folds, snapped it under his oxter as he stood up, touched his trilby in final salute, and then headed off with the hint of a limp through the midday traffic towards O'Meara's (now the Bachelor Inn).

As I crossed over to O'Connell Bridge in the noon sunlight, with one backward glance at O'Connell's burly figure and 'the most kindly and honest eyes that can be conceived', the story of D'Esterre sat easier with me than Ellen Courtenay's accusations. My narrator's tale had the true note of the man – the man of great visions and generous impulses.

The great width of O'Connell Bridge, as broad as it is long, gives a perspective to the quays. The present-day architectural poverty of one of the more adjacent quays, Bachelor's Walk (with its stretch of semi-demolished and shored up skeletons), is all the more noticeable by that fact. Formerly Carlisle Bridge, reconstructed and renamed in 1880, the bridge has never been afraid to 'show off' another kind of poverty, that of the supplicant beggar. And why should it? It straddles a river which flows through the very heart of a big-hearted city – a river of which it is said that whenever Dubliners participate in the traditional Liffey Swim (an annual one-and-a-quarter mile race from Watling Street Bridge to Butt Bridge) kindliness and charitable good nature may be skimmed off the surface of the water for a week after! What more strategic place for beggars to congregate?

An English writer in the last century once said, with meaningful exaggeration, that when he first saw the Dublin beggars it helped him solve the problem of what London beggars did with their cast-off clothes. It wasn't so much, I suspect, that the London poor were seldom as miserable as their Dublin counterparts. Frank and unashamed begging was frowned upon in London, even forbidden. The English mendicant – perhaps trying to retain a semblance of the national trait of 'keeping up appearances' – had only to make a show of plying some trade in order that the police should turn a blind eye. Every kind of hawking was tolerated: match-sellers, needle-and-pin vendors, sellers of every trifle under the sun, and, above all, musicians and buskers crowded the streets. In Dublin, while undoubtedly the same hawking was practised but where there has never been the need for pretence, nor a propensity for understatement, the unfortunate unashamedly pull out all the stops in a supreme effort to touch your heart and your pocket. I have been accosted and have invariably succumbed to the importunacies of Puck Fair tinkers, London down-and-outs, Roman 'professionals' and gypsies, but I venture to suggest that none had quite the same degree of expertise in the art of begging as those I remember from childhood on O'Connell Bridge. I recall a poor little woman, long since gone to a kinder place, who nonetheless scared us with her witch-like appearance and her manner of poking a thin, white Hansel-and-Gretel-like talon from out of the shadowy places of her voluminous black shawl with the words: 'May the blessin's of God an' His Holy Mother folly yeh to the ends of the earth', and then, depending on the pittance of farthings and halfpennies terrifyingly shoved into her emaciated claw, came either a half-hearted mumble of thanks or silence or worse, the cackling imprecation: 'and may the same blessin' never catch up on yo'r mean an' skinflint heart, blast yeh!' No wonder we scurried in giggling fear across the bridge and hurried up Westmoreland Street or D'Olier Street to the majesty of College Green and Grafton Street.

The first of the statues here is that of Thomas Moore at the junction of College Street and College Green. The poet Moore, once the populariser of Ireland's woes and the interpreter of its scenic beauty for the habitués of London salons which he loved to frequent, is no longer in fashion. It isn't solely that musical taste has changed so dramatically over the years. 'Tommy dearly loves a lord', Byron had once sneered at the 'potato-faced' Irishman (Moore's own description, not Byron's) and his convivial social climbing. To be fair, on another occasion Byron paid tribute to Moore as 'The poet of all circles and the idol of his own'. Dubliners, whose grandparents loved *Moore's Melodies* and who wouldn't dream of having a hooley without them, scarcely glance upwards nowadays at what Joyce described as Moore's 'servile head'. The wags, of course, still have their say, noting without ire that the author of 'The Meeting of the Waters' is perfectly situated above an underground toilet and that – in an age much given to amassing statistical data – the pen and notebook in his hand are for the purpose of keeping a tally on our urinations.

The liberal influence and ethos of their *alma mater* are discernible in the writings and speeches of the quartet of Irishmen whose statues stand outside Trinity College – Goldsmith and Burke inside the railings and flanking the main entrance, Grattan and Davis just across the road in College Green. Goldsmith must be everyone's favourite. Prior wrote: 'He was a man of an excellent heart and an amiable disposition'; Burke wept openly at the news of his death, so did most of his friends, including Dr Johnson, when 'their friend, their poet, their kind Goldsmith . . . the most generous of all men was dead within the black oak door' (Thackeray).

The smallpox, which scourged all Europe at that time, left the eight-year-old Goldsmith scarred and disfigured for life. He was pronounced a dunce. At Trinity he was chastised by his tutor for throwing a hooley in his rooms and took the smack on the ear so much to heart that he pawned his few books and belongings and disappeared from college, friends and family. He made a vagabond tour of Europe, was a strolling player, an apothecary's assistant, a school usher, a vagrant. When he turned up in London, aged twenty-eight, the history of this genial and improvident Irishman consisted mainly of anecdotes of failures, disappointments and roistering. And then (let Thackeray take up the tale) 'After years of dire struggle, and neglect and poverty, his heart turning back as fondly to his native place as it had longed eagerly for change when sheltered there, he writes a book and a poem, full of the recollections and feelings of home: he paints the friends and scenes of his youth, and peoples Auburn and Wakefield with remembrances of Lissoy. Wander he must, but he carries away a home-relic with him, and dies with it on his breast.' And Scott adds: 'We read *The*

Vicar of Wakefield in youth and in age – we return to it again and again, and bless the memory of an author who contrives so well to reconcile us to human nature.'

In a letter written in 1746, while he was a student in Trinity, Burke says, 'All my studies have rather proceeded from sallies of passion than from the preference of sound reason.' Those sallies of passion, allied to the sound reason of maturity, produced splendid orations in an age famous for its oratory. All the great political questions of the age fired the imagination of a statesman who never ceased to be a poet. Yet even when he was the mainstay of his party the honours bestowed on Burke were few, and the services of 'the greatest orator of his day' were niggardly rewarded.

The greatest orator? Ah, but that was only in a London parliament which was outshone by its Dublin offspring where Grattan and Flood – yes, and even Sir Boyle Roche with his herd of Irish bulls! – were raising oratory to new and brilliant levels. That Irish parliament (housed in what is now the Bank of Ireland) was unique in that it was the only such assembly ever to vote itself out of existence, for a price, admittedly. It all began when London was prepared to offer a going rate of 2,000 guineas plus a pension or salary to all who voted against the rebellious American colonies in the 1770s. There were sufficient takers. Against one such taker, Grattan inveighed: 'He stands with a metaphor in his mouth and a bribe in his pocket!' It ended when the bribe-takers voted their parliament into extinction with the Act of Union thirty years later. Ireland, always a poor country, was ever a rich one to sell. What a squalid tale it is. Grattan's statue:

With hand held high, has coldly turned his back
On the one and only parliament to give itself the sack.
He faces Ned and Noll (as if round village pump)
And lambastes the dirty lousers who sold out for the
'lump'.
'For they voted in the Union, in return for gold and rank
And Henry Grattan's parliament was auctioned to a
bank!'

The Thomas Davis Memorial commemorates one of the founder members of *The Nation* newspaper and the most prolific of the 'Young Ireland' poets, whose patriotic verses graced its pages in the heady 'Repeal of the Act of Union' days of the early 1840s. Selling 10,000 copies, *The Nation's* exuberant mixture of political comment, social enquiry, literary features and stirring poetry had an instant appeal, even though its exorbitant price of sixpence a copy meant that most readers had to borrow it from news-vendors at a penny an hour! The pacifist O'Connell, wary of its firebrand politics, prophesied that it would soon burn itself out. It did, but only when most of its founder members and some of its contributors were rounded up after the Young Ireland rebellion of 1848. Davis, having died a couple of years earlier at the age of thirty-one, wasn't around to see the result of his fiery and inspiring poetry. The newspaper managed to linger on until the 1880s – long enough to provide employment for a stereotyper foreman and radical emigré, displaced by the Italian Risorgimento wars, named Giuseppe Caprani (my great-grandfather). 'Today, all that remains of the great outpouring of patriotic energy that created *The Nation*, apart from the slumbering file copies, is a small metal plaque on the front wall of Independent House in Middle Abbey Street, recording the fact that the site once housed the offices of *The Nation*' (Hugh Oram, *The Newspaper Book*, 1983).

Davis's bronze statue on its nine-foot block of granite and the ground-level acolytes representing Ireland's four provinces, 'trumpeting' water back into the pool, stand on the site once occupied by the proud equestrian statue of William of Orange. If statues have souls – I'm inclined to think they do – then King Billy's must have been the most befuddled and baffled effigy in all of Christendom. For more than 200 years – the work of Grinling Gibbons, it was unveiled in 1701 on the anniversary of the Battle of the Boyne – it was annually venerated by Orangemen, who decorated it with lilies, and abused by Jacobites, Catholics, Nationalists and Republicans, who regularly daubed and defaced it. It was almost certainly the first Dublin statue to be 'blasted'. In 1836 a gunpowder mutilation caused the Surgeon-General, Sir Philip Crampton, to dash to the scene on receipt of an urgent message explaining how a most 'important personage had fallen from his horse outside the Bank of Ireland'. Its sufferings continued until

1929 when (in the words of a very good friend of mine) 'my father and some of his comrades finally blew it up and then hid in a nearby bakery till the dust had settled'.

The lineal mental descendants of those Trinity students of yore, who either bedecked 'King William of glorious memory' with lilies, or bedaubed with black paint 'Protestant Billy' and his innocent charger, still express their Rag Week enthusiasms by occasionally pouring washing-up liquids into the Thomas Davis pool and creating a soapy bubbledom in the middle of College Green. And what of poor, gentle Davis? In youth he longed to fall in battle – so much more glorious than to be quietly buried by a vicar! – but ill-health robbed him of that old age which knows it's the impulse of a fool or an idealist to think one form of death better than another. Davis's best-known song, 'A Nation Once Again', is still sung lustily by Dubliners – especially at the curfew hour in pubs – even if most of us (no less than Davis or our political leaders of today) haven't quite made up our minds on the matter of what sort of nation it should be. Perhaps that's why we are happier belting out a harmless, non-partisan rendition of 'Molly Malone'?

The good lady's statue stands where Grafton Street is intersected by Nassau and Suffolk streets, another millenial addition to the pantheon of Dublin worthies. Such an effigy was long overdue, not only because it introduces a female – and an attractively buxom one at that! – into the long line of politicos and poets with their outstretched, raised and declamatory hands, but because it gives a kind of plebeian 'it's-in-our-blood' balance to the streetscape. Molly, with her wheelbarrow (presumably of winkles, potted herrings, cockles and mussels), is 'one of us', at eye level, requiring no lofty column or raised plinth, no surrounding angels or magnificent heraldry. She's someone you casually bump into on your stroll, like the jaunty Joyce at North Earl Street looking uncommonly pleased with himself, or the Two Shoppers seated outside the Woollen Mills at the Ha'penny Bridge end of Liffey Street. And you're all the richer for the experience.

Little is known of Molly's life or the ballad's origin. During the Millenium year a researcher claimed to have discovered her death certificate in old parish records and suggested that she most probably died not from 'the fever', but from venereal disease, mischeviously hinting at activities other than wheeling her barrow through streets broad and narrow. How dare he impugn our heroine's honour! We dismiss the imputation of loose living out of hand. On what does he base it? Certainly VD was rife during the eighteenth century, though not nearly so prevalent as typhus. The slums stank and there were no sewers; as late as the early 1800s the areas in front of the stately townhouses of Gardiner's Mall were awash with household refuse and sewage. The all-pervasive 'Liffey Fever' was a catch-all phrase for every ill emanating from overcrowded hovels, insanitation, filth and tainted foodstuffs. The development of Dublin port at the time meant an end to the once-flourishing oyster beds at Poolbeg, and contamination from domestic sewage forced the closure of similar beds at Clontarf, Sutton and Malahide. It is far more likely that our heroine died of typhus from eating tainted seafood, rather than the promiscuousness of her amours.

Be that as it may the song to her memory has a world-wide resonance. It is said that the popularity of a traditional ballad may be gauged by the types who sing it and by the frequency and the locations of its renditions. Dublin's anthem 'Cockles and Mussels' (yet another favourite from the pen of that ubiquitous and prolific poet Anon) is sung everywhere. Indeed, I myself claim the dubious distinction of having translated it into a kind of pidgin Italian for the famed Alpine male choristers of *Coro Penna Nera*, and my Lombardian friends tell me that oft in the stilly night the groves around Samarate echo to the sonorous harmonies of '*A Dublino ci sono le fanciulle belle*'. It is one of those airs more often sung by trained singers, choral groups, dance-band vocalists and raucous football fans than by 'pure' ballad singers, but that doyen of Dublin traditional singers, my friend Frank Harte, says: 'Just because such a great song has fallen on hard times and mixed in the above company for too long, it should not be neglected by the unaccompanied singer.'

Molly's statue is the start of the real Grafton Street. I am keenly sensitive to streets. With their stone, brick, plate glass and shopfronts they pretend to be impersonal and rarely succeed. I seldom walk a Dublin street without wondering how it looked in Swift's day, or if Goldsmith stood at such a corner, quietly mingling with the motley crowd to watch the effect of his rhyming words on the audience (while at Trinity, he wrote ballads for the street singers, who paid him a crown for a poem, and his pleasure was to steal out at night and hear his verses sung). But Grafton Street doesn't really lend itself to musings on a vanished age. It is too vibrantly alive. It is, much more, I think, than O'Connell Street, a street of today. Its reminders of the past are muted, almost concealed. For Dubliners and visitors alike, Grafton Street represents the top notch, whether in jewellery, fashion or fancy goods.

And Grafton's Street's buskers are the top notch: Paddy 'Bones' Sweeney, with his harmonica and bodhran, the miming Diceman, Frank Quinlan and his guitar, the young bardic poet Tierney, the puppeteers and blink-a-blonk banjo men – all setting up an intimate rapport with the people gathered round them. The street always strikes a cheerful, carnival note, never ceasing to delight as it works slowly up towards St Stephen's Green like a drama working up towards its climax and then ending with a great flourish before the Fusiliers' Archway entrance to the Green.

· 4 ·

St Stephen's Green

I SELDOM walk into the Green without feeling that each curving pathway through the shrubbery and trees will bring me face to face with a new discovery, a splendid adventure. This may have something to do with the fact that my earliest recollection of the Green goes back to when, as a four- or five-year old happily feeding the ducks (and eagerly stretching out my piece of stale bread to ensure that at least one little duckling on the fringe of the group got his fair share), I suddenly tumbled bum-over-tip into the pond. My mother, panic-stricken and fully clothed, instantly jumped in after me. There was great excitement as I spluttered to the surface for the second time, and no end of helping hands for 'Oh-Jayz-Mary-'n-Joseph, the pore woman an' the chile!' The onlookers quickly hauled us in. They proferred odds and ends of dry clothing, they fashioned makeshift towels, they produced ice-cream and biscuits, they commiserated, they laughed – they turned 'disaster' into a funny adventure. Everywhere good nature and relief asserted itself. It was a lovely sunny day. I recall nothing of the sodden aftermath nor of my mother's discomfiture on the homeward bus.

Ever since, the phrase 'the Green' has retained the echo of a merry splash of water and sunlight, of friendly faces and laughter. And notice, too, the significant name: 'the Green'. Every other park and square in the city is known as the so-and-so park or the such-and-such square. But this city-centre oasis of flower-beds, duck-pond, shrubbery and lawns is simply and affectionately known as the Green. It is like the centre-piece of some rural village, incapable of confusion with any other place. Almost everyone refers to it thus.

Those who decline to do so and prefer its more correct appelations were (especially in the past, where such things seemed to matter) strongly suspected of being 'religionists' – Prods invariably called it Stephen's Green, good Catholics always prefixed Saint. By the same token we were expected to differentiate between those who spoke of 26 December as Boxing Day instead of St Stephen's Day – and one wonders now what that early martyr for the Christian faith might think of his name being used later in connection with petty Christian devisiveness? One also wonders how this ancient sward – once a late medieval public common (with all the rude, and sometimes brutal, revelry that the term implies), often a gibbet and gallows green, once a promenade for rakes and profligates, later a haunt for whores and bawds – should come to bear the saint's name? Perhaps, in truth, because he is the patron of all such unfortunates?

The ancient common became a municipally owned square of twenty-seven acres (including its stone wall, ditch and surrounding muddy roadway) in the 1660s. The adjoining eighty-odd lots were apportioned among the town's most influential gentlemen, aldermen, merchants, property speculators and respectable tradesmen so that 'wast lands about this cittie, that now addeth nothing at all to pleasure or profitt' might be set to good use. Gradually, over the next seventy or eighty years, and especially in the 1740s when the Duke of Leinster defied the taunts of Dublin's fashionable northside by building the city's finest mansion, Leinster House, in rural pasture land close by the ancient common, St Stephen's Green came into its own. The gentry followed the duke's example. The Green soon had its 'Beaux Walk', a handsome promenade for fops, periwigged dandies and devil-may-care young bucks like Bishop Whaley's son who once jumped out of his father's sedate townhouse window (for a wager, naturally!) to kiss the first pretty girl passing by in a carriage. For another such wager the bishop's harum-scarum son walked all the way to the Holy Land and back, thus earning his sobriquet 'Jerusalem' Whaley, which helped to distinguish him from his virulently anti-papist pater known as 'Burn-Chapel' Whaley.

Following the Act of Union, when the political and social hub of Ireland was wrenched to London and Westminster (via Holyhead), the Green still retained its aura of fashionable pleasance and townhouse elegance. The rural magnates and provincial landlords – while freed of the costly upkeep of their Dublin mansions now that the Irish parliament had ceased to exist – still required for short periods the same degree of luxury when journeying back and forth through Dublin to Westmeath or West Cork from distant Westminster. An acceptable substitute for the former family townhouse proved to be a large, comfortable hotel replete with elegant drawing-rooms, private apartments, handsome foyers and staircases, good food, fires burning cheerfully night and day, and a few of one's former servants still on hand to attend to one's needs with just that correct degree of servility and deference that suited the transformation from old retainer to new status of hotelier.

The houses of the aristocrats were quickly passing into the hands of the commercial classes, and the hotel trade was booming. Wright's *Guide to Dublin 1821* lists twenty-seven upper-class hotels calculated to attract the type of guest desiring the ambience of an old townhouse allied to the conveniences of a 'modern' hotel, and all of them (not to mention cheaper, lesser-class inns and boarding-houses) were situated in a smallish city hemmed in by the two canals north and south, and Kingsbridge and Trinity west and east. Six of these 'spacious and respectable' hotels were in Sackville (now O'Connell) Street, the most notable being that of an ex-butler named Tom Gresham. A typical bill of the time – four nights, full board, sherry and Madeira with dinner – worked out at one pound, fourteen shillings and one-and-a-half pence!

On the other side of the Liffey Martin Burke's Shelbourne Hotel, Stephen's Green, held sway. Burke purchased three adjoining houses on the north side of the Green – one of the trio being the more prominent Shelbourne House, not long after it had been used as a torture barracks by the sadistic and well-named 'Walking Gallows' Hempenstall in the aftermath of the 1798 Rebellion – and the purchase of the site happily coincided with the introduction of the new and wondrous gas-lighting to Dublin. The new-fangled piped gas, like that even greater time-saving innovation of a decade later – that cancatenation of mind-boggling, horseless, steam-driven coaches snorting and puffing smartly out from Westland Row to Kingstown Harbour – was 'bound to come', according to those perennial experts, the Dublin know-alls.

And the Gresham and the Shelbourne were not only on hand to gracefully see out the demise of one leisurely age, but to witness the triumphant emergence of a new era. Still happily with us in this jet age, and on their original sites (though with understandable rebuilding, additions and accretions), both hotels are links with the age of mail coach 'four-in-hands' and puffing billies. The Gresham and Upper Sackville Street was the great departure point for northbound coaches, the Shelbourne was the southside departure place for coaches to Wicklow, Wexford and Waterford. They are reminders of a time, according to some later experts, when it was usual for coach passengers to appoint a chairman 'among themselves at the beginning of the journey, and it was decided by vote whether stops should be made at any inns, and which' (Mervyn Tregaskis, 'The Romance of the Road', *Fry's Magazine*, 1908).

Thus, the thirty-six miles to Arklow might be achieved in three-and-a-half hours (the old coach-and-four averaged about ten miles per hour) or might take twice as long, depending on the voting and how many taverns along the way offered additional enticements. One hesitates to think of the problems confronting some impatient merchant, commercial traveller anxious to make contact with a client, or abstemious spinster, all hoping to reach their respective destinations before nightfall and who happened to fall into the company of a majority of convivial topers and good trenchermen!

All of this is the history of a vanished age, the reminders of which may be glimpsed in the presence of the 'resurrected' jarvies with their fast little ponies who now once again cater for the tourists from the Shelbourne. It is a most heartening development for those of us who grew up in an age when there was still almost as much horse-drawn as motor traffic and when the smell of horse manure was as much a part of the street and as widespread as today's petrol fumes.

For today's beautifully landscaped Green with its formal lawns, flower-beds, fountains, wooded walks, bandstand, rustic bridge and duck-pond (fed by the waters of the Grand Canal), we are indebted to the munificence of Sir Arthur Guinness, who, in 1877, had the largely derelict and overgrown site transformed and opened to the public. Another nearby Guinness gift to the nation was Iveagh House (now the offices of the Department of Foreign Affairs) at the south-east corner of the Green – and when someone once remarked to Brendan Behan how good the Guinness dynasty had been to the city of Dublin he riposted with the reminder that considering the partiality of the citizens for porter over the preceding 200 years, 'Dubliners have been very good to the Guinness family.' Be that as it may, Sir Arthur turned a field into an open-air museum: the Green (a quarter-mile long on each of its four sides) contains fifteen monuments and statues. The very first one, erected in 1758, was a bronze equestrian statue to George II and – yes, you've guessed it! – was blasted from its base in the wee hours of a May morning in 1937. The flower-bed that now marks the spot is no mean apology for the outrage.

My favourite entrance to the Green is, after walking up Grafton Street, to pass under the Fusiliers' Arch and come into a place of bosky tints. Left and right lie transepts of dappled lawn, wooded walks and bird song, a place of strange harmony with the arch's sad splendour of sacrifice. The monument was formally opened in 1907 by the Duke of Connaught as a memorial to the officers and men of the five battalions of the Royal Dublin Fusiliers who fell in the Boer War. Scarcely noticed – hardly even a gaping place for today's bevy of typists, office-workers and shoppers passing to and fro under the curved panels inscribed with the 200-odd names of the fallen and forgotten – the arch says nothing of the horrors of war, though local names like Byrne and Cullen and the battlefields of Tugela Heights, Hartshill and Ladysmith have tears in them. We are perhaps too far away from that war which ushered in the twentieth century, and the undreamt of beastliness of that century's subsequent wars, for us to interpret it today. Yet, as much as any of the other soldierly monuments in the city, this has a deep poignancy for me, perhaps because of the whisper of wind in the nearby trees and the echoing footsteps of strolling lovers under the archway. Had they lived, many of the fusiliers would surely have strolled with their sweethearts through the Green, and we might even have known them in their old age. The mind weeps a little at the thought of the 235 Dubs who lie in the soil of the veldt which is forever Ireland.

As a child I once overheard someone in a Dublin street say in a kind of hushed aside, 'There's the Bugler Dunne!' Heads turned, people nodded. I was either too small, or unconcerned, to catch a glimpse of the object of their sudden interest and might have dismissed the matter entirely from my mind but for the fact that the speaker's tone had that awe-filled, or proud, intonation which even then I was beginning to learn was invariably reserved for those 'street celebrities' of the day – men like the popular Lord Mayor Alfie Byrne, boxer Jack Doyle, comedian Jimmy O'Dea or Nolan the prison-escaper. Many years later, in my mid-teens, I was halted beneath the Fusiliers' Arch, reading through the names of the dead, when an old-timer briefly paused beside me and muttered: 'Only for the Bugler Dunne there'd be twice as many names up there and they would've havin' to build a monument double the size, so they would!' And before I could question him he was gone, marching into the Grafton Street crowds with that shoulders-straight, chin-up gait that one associates with old soldiers.

But who was the Bugler Dunne? Over the years I picked up snippets of a tale that might have come straight out of the pages of *The Boy's Own Adventure* magazine or from one of A. G. Henty's novels, many of which (though often tattered and dog eared) were still being swopped and passed around in our boyhood as fine examples of stories 'full of action from first page to last; they are clean, and they exalt physical and moral courage'. Henty's youthful heroes were invariably drummer-boys in the army of the Raj, Jim Hawkins-like stowaways on Nelson's men-o'-war, scouts for *Buller in Natal* or with *Kitchener in the Sudan*, *Gordon at Khartoum* and *Clive in India*. But how did a Dubliner like Dunne fit into this category? About twelve years ago I was favoured with the loan of some valuable old press cuttings, photos and Edwardian postcards from a relative of Bugler Dunne's, and, briefly, this is the story that emerged from such memorabilia.

In December 1899, and in what became known as the black week of the South African War when the British army was reeling from a succession of swift defeats at the hands of the Boers, General Sir Redvers Buller advanced to attack the Boers, strongly entrenched at Colenso on the Tugela River. The attack was delivered across an open plain, with the river and the heights beyond. General Hart's Irish Brigade advanced in quarter column to a loop in the river where they attempted to cross. From the heights the Boers opened fire. Caught in mid-stream, confusion quickly reigned when from somewhere a bugle sounded the retreat. It was then that the fifteen-year-old boy bugler with the advancing Dublin Fusiliers saved the day. He alone knew that as no officer had commanded him to sound 'Retreat', the sound must be coming from the Boer positions as a ruse to cause the very confusion now reigning. Without waiting for orders Dunne raised his trumpet to his lips and blasted out 'Advance'. His comrades steadied, rallied, turned and pressed forward. Louder and louder, never faltering, the bugler urged the Dubs onwards. With their ploy discovered the Boer sharpshooters tried to pick off the brave youngster. A bullet smashed into his instrument, wrenching it from his grip and sending it splashing down into the stream. He went in after it and came up spluttering out the notes of defiance. The Boers gradually fell back – and what might have been a disastrous rout at the loop in the river became a partial victory. It was different elsewhere; of Buller's overall force of 20,000 men over 1,000 were killed, wounded or missing, and eight artillery pieces captured. A profound impression was created in Britain by the news of these defeats following so closely on each other. A morale booster was urgently needed.

The war correspondents had picked up the story of the gallant boy bugler and how, when questioned later by superior officers, he'd naively stated that, as it was his first time under fire, he naturally took it that there would be an order to advance because his father (a career sergeant with the Fusiliers) had always told him that the 'Dublin Fusiliers never retreat'. It was the stuff of romance and just what the occasion required. The buglar was decorated, dispatched back to London, received at Buckingham Palace by the ageing Queen Victoria, who presented him with a new silver-plated bugle, and then was toured around the British music-hall circuit with his 'bugle act' as part of an army recruitment drive. He served again in the 1914–18 War and later became a merchant seaman. The events – the awful carnage and the unending heroism – of the Great War gradually eclipsed his Boer War deed from the public gaze, though in later years, as a seaman, he was to discover in places as far apart as Australia and Canada that there was more than one imposter who turned up at annual South African war-veterans reunions claiming to be the authentic boy bugler of the Tugela River! Such masquerading amused him. Dunne retired from the merchant navy in his fifties, settled down in his native Dublin and died in 1955 – a quiet, dignified old man who had seen too much of war and the world to be affected by the street murmers of: 'There's the Bugler Dunne!' In the absence of any commemorative plaque to his memory (so far as I know) I cannot help but think that the Fusiliers' Arch is as much a monument to his quick thinking and bravery as to his fallen comrades – 'Only for the Bugler Dunne there'd be twice as many names up there.'

If I have a preferential entrance to the Green, then a reluctance to quit it denies me any favourite exit point. However, if I must be off and am not tied to any strict timetable, I usually try to maintain the mood induced by wood, grass and flowers by heading off in the direction of nearby Merrion Square, a bishop's private park now thrown open to the public. This normally entails exiting at the Shelbourne corner with the adjoining Huguenot cemetery dating from 1693. Almost next door to the cemetery, at 2 and 3 Merrion Row, once stood the popular Swiss Chalet Café where, about 1951, I attended one of my first dances or 'hops' in the company of my fellow printing apprentices. One of them introduced us to a trio of very attractive, demure, dark-eyed 'foreign-looking' girls and later told us that, 'No, they're as Dublin as the rest of us. Protestants, though. They get their dark hair and complexion from their Huguenot ancestry, you see.'

Sometimes, when passing the old cemetery and the place where the Swiss Chalet stood (boarded up for many years it was demolished about 1977), I muse on the 'fabric of Dublin-ness'. If there is any truth in the contention that all persons draw from their native districts certain predispositions, then our ancestors – Gaels, Vikings, Cambro-Normans, Anglo-Irish, Dutch Reformists, Flemings, Walloons, French Huguenots, German Palatines, Scots, Portuguese and Baltic Jews, Italians – must have infused the melting pot by the Liffey with some of the best qualities of an ancient homeland, for resilience, good humour, wit and hospitality are said to be among the primary characteristics of Dubliners. Boastfulness is another, I suppose, for we always maintain a perfect right to describe our own virtues!

Much of that racy imperturbability and earthy wit, immortalised in ballad form and nightly emanating from O'Donoghue's Pub just opposite the old Swiss Chalet, launched the international music careers of the Furey Brothers, Ronnie Drew, Luke Kelly and the Dubliners et al. And the good patron of O'Donoghue's, Mr Hynes (like most of the publicans in the inner city), never once forbade any of us unknown scribblers with our 'nixered' broadsheets and rowdy rhymes from hawking our apprentice offerings among the practitioners of pipe, fiddle and banjo or their many listeners. With beer to buy and the needs of a pass-round cap to meet, they rarely had cash for our atrocious doggerels! And we were completely unaware that we were actually among that brotherhood of balladeers ranging from the barely literate and legendary Zozimus to luminaries of the English language like Goldsmith and Lever (the latter, in his student days, went about the city in a hired theatrical uniform singing his own compositions). We were enriched by our impecunious sorties into the singing pubs; we sold shag-all and learned much. What memories this short street – little more than the frontage to an old cemetery, two fine pubs, the entrance to the Treasury Gallery of the National Museum, a florist-cum-hardware shop, and the courtyard doorway to Commendatore Sidoli's excellent Unicorn Restaurant where Franco Macchi, Marco Luoni and the Alpine choristers sang 'Il Piave Mormoro', 'La Penna Nera' and 'Me Compare Giacometto' and invited Mary and I to join them in 'La Montanera' – holds for me.

By the by, Preston Street (off Amiens Street, and where my good friends John and Ruth Breslin until very recently had their excellent printery and 'refuge for the floating chapel' of unemployed printers) now claims to be the shortest street in Dublin, with only four hall-doors. Until the mid 1960s, Canon Street (off Bride Street, in the Liberties) held the title. Named after the minor canons of St Patrick's Cathedral, Canon Street had only one address, that of Rutledge's Public House. It was also the venue for the Dublin bird market, a Sunday morning trading place for caged singing birds – canaries, linnets, redpolls, goldfinches, budgies and cross-bred 'mules' – most certainly dating back to Huguenot times (though some authorities claim it originated with the first Norman invaders and is thus one of the oldest such markets in the world). Since the Protection of Animals Act of 1965, it is now removed to a private yard off nearby Peter Street. Short streets lead to long digressions! I think I was on my way to Merrion Square.

The healthfulness of the Irish capital is doubtless partly due to its fresh winds coming in from the bay with their salty tang or down from the heathery mountains, and to its many large parks and open spaces. Fitzwilliam Square, St Stephen's Green, Herbert Park and Merrion Square were once the preserve of the upper classes. One after another, they have been thrown open to *hoi polloi*. In Victorian times the offspring of aristocratic and respectable mercantile families were given their daily airings, accompanied by their nannies, in Merrion Square. Later, with their own private latchkeys, they entered the park and played tennis or croquet. The lower classes were rigorously excluded and could merely peer through the bars of the high iron railings. Until, in 1849 (when areas of the city became vast refugee camps for victims of the Great Famine), the famous French chef Alexis Soyer and his team were sent over to Dublin to establish their open-air soup kitchens for the limping throngs seeking work or seeking foreign boats. Merrion Square was opened to the multitudes. Soyer set up his soup-dispensing depot on the tennis grounds. The great national tragedy allied to well-meaning though belated middle-class charitableness flung open the gates and the latchkeys were redundant for a year or two. In the post-Famine era they were quickly dusted off and restored to their original use for more than a century.

Meanwhile, Merrion Square's park – though not the surrounding and valuable house property, naturally – had fallen into the hands of the Roman Catholic Archbishop of Dublin who had plans to build a magnificent cathedral on the site (and here it is interesting to note that no Catholic bishop of Dublin has ever petitioned the Roman Pontiff to revoke the cathedral status of Christ Church, which, since the Reformation, has been under the care of the Church of Ireland). Until the Act of Catholic Emancipation of 1829, Catholic churches – such as Marlborough Street's Pro-Cathedral (meaning a kind of temporary or substitute cathedral) – were generally relegated to side streets in order to avoid offending the Protestant 'powers-that-be' with too great a display of ostentation or growing confidence. The Merrion Square park cathedral was intended to remedy all that. But it never came to pass – after a century of ownership Archbishop Ryan generously handed over the park to Dublin Corporation in 1974 for the use of the citizens. The latchkey era was finally over. Perhaps the good and popular Dermot Ryan knew that Dublin might have had a church too many? Certainly, to judge by a skyline attractively punctuated with steeples, church towers, spires and domes, the city is an eminently religious metropolis – but to let the eye drop to a street level of neon-lit slot-machine joints and fast-food takeaways is to know that Mammon prevails. The citizens – and their children especially – are no longer eager to worship at the former and if they are to be protected from the worst excesses of the latter, then there is a great need for green sanctuaries of peace. I suspect that Bishop Ryan intuitively recognised this truth.

The park (officially named after Bishop Ryan, a native Dubliner) is everything a city-centre refuge should be: a kiddies' playground, a beautifully landscaped garden, a site for sculptures, a quiet retreat, a lunch-hour haven for harassed office-workers – and with trees, shrubs and delightful flower-gardens, the park forms an extremely attractive perspective for viewing the surrounding Georgian houses and musing on their history and former occupants. Sir Jonah Barrington, Daniel O'Connell, Joseph Sheridan Le Fanu, W. B. Yeats and the Wildes all lived here.

There are ghosts here, too – dark hauntings of retribution and regret. And a curious Huguenot echo, or thread, links them together. Le Fanu was born in 1814, the son of a clergyman of Huguenot extraction. Around the same time another clergyman of Huguenot extraction, Charles Maturin (the eccentric curate at St Peter's), wrote *Melmoth the Wanderer*, one of the earliest and most successful of nineteenth-century 'horror' stories. In 1824 Maturin died at his home in York Street where he used to keep the shutters closed most days and write 'and dance about' the place by artificial light. His terror novels must have impressed themselves on Le Fanu's young mind. Pritchett says: 'Le Fanu's imagination was fed by things that must have lain hidden and still lie in the Dublin unconscious', for he abandoned his legal profession for a writing career and in turn gave Victorian readers the first great Vampire story, *Carmilla*. His ghost stories and novels, such as *The House by the Churchyard*, are full of sinister whisperings and secret guilts. After the death of his wife in 1858 Le Fanu shut himself up in his house, 70 Merrion Square South, and became so much of a recluse that not even his life-long friend and fellow-writer Charles Lever was permitted to visit him. Until his lonely death fifteen years later, Le Fanu wrote his macabre tales here, only occasionally venturing out at dusk to walk with solemn tread under the dripping trees of the park.

The death of Sir William Wilde at 1 Merrion Square North reads like something from one of Le Fanu's stories. Wilde was one of the most colourful and versatile men of his era: a successful ophthalmologist, surgeon to Queen Victoria (from whom he received his knighthood), a bestselling travel writer, topographer, founder-editor of two respected medical journals, archaeologist, antiquarian and founder of St Mark's Hospital (later amalgamated with another hospital as the Royal Victoria Eye and Ear Hospital). Dr Wilde married Maturin's niece, Jane Francesca Elgee, the daughter of a Wexford clergyman. Under the pen-name 'Speranza' Jane wrote rousing if, by today's standards, unreadable poetry and fiery patriotic articles for *The Nation*, one of which landed the editor Charles Gavan Duffy in jail. Together the Wildes reigned over Dublin's Bohemian mini-world, lavishly entertaining and giving boisterous parties at their Merrion Square salon. But the brilliant doctor was also rumoured to be a notorious philanderer. One of his mistresses – or victims? – published a pamphlet accusing him of having seduced her while she was under the influence of drugs administered by him in his surgery. She hired newsboys to sell the 'tell-all' leaflets outside his crowded lecture hall. Strangely prefiguring the scandal and tragedy that later doomed his celebrated son Oscar, Dr Wilde took a libel action. It resulted in an award of a farthing in damages to the lady, and in the fashionable doctor taking to heavy drinking and even heavier quarrelling with his ever-decreasing circle of friends, patients, colleagues and students. He went downhill rapidly.

Years later, on his deathbed, he was visited by his accuser. Heavily and mysteriously veiled, she would silently enter the house and make her way upstairs. No one stopped her or ever questioned her. She was permitted to come and go during those final days without hindrance, to sit wordlessly by his bed for hours, to gaze down through the swathing veil into the dull and uncomprehending eyes of the dying man. As soon as he was dead and in his coffin she was gone, silently and mysteriously vanishing into the night, never to be seen again. Who was she? What impelled her eerie vigil: gloating revenge, regret, retribution? Was it a twisted and unrequitted passion? It is a tale that ends with all the obsessive secrecy of one of Le Fanu's macabre masterpieces.

There are evenings when walking through Merrion Square – usually November evenings, when figures emerge swiftly from the shadowy mist and into the glow of street lamps and then just as quickly disappear again – one hears footsteps following in the dark. Whose footsteps? Ghosts? Or are they only the echoes of our own hurrying, quietly haunting us with old tales? Yes, Merrion Square and its beautiful park are best visited on a bright spring morning when the air has the freshness and substance of heady wine.

· 5 ·

Phoenix Park

When I worked as a journeyman letterpress machineman in the printing department of London's Savoy Hotel in 1959, one of my Cockney work-mates, doubtlessly thinking he was helping a homesick Paddy to 'acclimatise' (and kindly suggesting weekend recreations, places of interest and sight-seeing strolls for myself and my young bride), at one stage listed all his city's broad and leafy parks for our delectation: Regent's Park, Hyde Park, Kensington Gardens, St James's Park, Battersea Park and Greenwich Park. He added that all had been royal preserves in bygone days but that various British monarchs over the years had magnanimously opened them to the public. Rather ungraciously, I suppose (and with what I know now to have been a youthful chauvinism), I responded with the information that in my hometown we had similar municipal parks and that our major one – once an ancient plain and public common that had been hijacked by the minions of a foreign king and turned into a royal deer park – could quite easily fit all his London parks into its vast extent of 1,752 acres. For good measure I threw in the fact that our Mansion House predated his by about fifteen years.

He didn't, of course, believe me on either count. Why should he? London was the centre of his world. Dublin was mine. I had no encyclopedia on hand to prove my argument. I was armed only with the handed-down truths of that trivia which is the gospel of all true Dubliners: that we are no less than London, and in some respects we are better. While subsequent readings and casual researches proved my long-ago boast to have been correct, the experience of the intervening years has shown me that the churlish sensitivity of a provincial more than thirty years ago misconstrued that kindly, cheery Cockney helpfulness, which it has always been my good fortune to receive, then and on all later visits to our sister-capital on the Thames.

Occasionally over those same years I've wondered what Bert Hocking, Frankie Westrop, Alf Trunkie and Charlie Pink – names that have the unmistakable ring of Bow Bells and Widdicombe Fair, and as such could never easily fit in with Dublin nomenclature – and my other old London workmates would have thought of our Phoenix Park. Thirty-five years ago no other city of comparable size anywhere in the world could boast a completely enclosed park of seven-miles circumference containing the official residence of the nation's president; the residences of the American ambassador and the Papal Nuncio; a 'wilderness' with a herd of 400 free-ranging fallow deer; cricket and polo fields; a city hospital; a rivulet and a scattering of woodlands, glens and hills; a world-famous zoo dating from 1831 (notable for the breeding of lions in captivity); a People's Park; a Cheshire home; eight large ponds (one with an island, another with a skaters' rink – whenever there's ice!); a Papal Cross and Mass field dating from the pontifical visit of 1979; a magazine (or arsenal) dating from the eighteenth century; an understated 'Fifteen Acres' of soccer, Gaelic football and hurling fields; a 'Hollow' glen for military band recitals (and surrounding shrubbery for courting couples); the government's Department of Defence; the headquarters of the Ordnance Survey; a major racecourse; a schoolhouse; the city's only remaining gas lamps; the headquarters of the Garda Siochana; the Civil Defence school; the extensive army and police athletic grounds; and Dublin's tallest monument – and all of this encompassed within a stone boundary wall punctuated by eight main gates which are linked with interconnecting roadways well known to the city's motorists, cyclists, horse-riders and pedestrians. 'Sure, where would you get the like?' as Dubliners frequently say when trying to cloak pride in such wonders with an offhand, even deprecatory, remark. Where indeed!

I wonder, too, what my erstwhile and prosaic London mates of yore would have thought of our idiosyncratic penchant for misnomers. The Phoenix Park contains quite a few. For a start, it owes its name to a curious corruption of the Gaelic word *uisge*, in this case *fionn uisge*, meaning 'clear water' (a reference to an ancient chalybeate mineral spa close by the present zoo). The thirty-foot Phoenix Monument (erected in 1747 by Viceroy Lord Chesterfield, who did so much to beautify and develop the park during his tenure) depicts the mythical bird rising from its flames, but it has been known to generations of Dubliners as the Eagle. The extensive plain known to all and sundry as the Fifteen Acres (the largest of the open spaces and once a duelling ground) contains well in excess of a hundred acres. Of the eight entrances to the park, the main one, known as Parkgate, is the only one that for as long as I can remember never had a gate.

This fashion for misnomers, or a sense of fun akin to them, may have started with Dean Swift. When the Earl of Wharton (reputed to be the author of the rousing song 'Lillibullero', which is said to have done more to dethrone James II than all that monarch's ham-fisted politics) was Viceroy in the early 1700s, he decided to build a massive magazine, or military ammunition storehouse, on Thomas's Hill in the park. Swift, sensing a chance for a little political satire, wrote:

> Behold a proof of Irish sense;
> Here Irish wit is seen;
> When nothing's left that's worth defence
> We build a magazine.

That grim-looking magazine fort is still a fine example of eighteenth-century defensive architecture. On its hill-top perch above Islandbridge Gate it has unrestricted views for miles on all sides, and its stout granite, gun-turreted walls were once surrounded by a water-filled moat above which stood a drawbridge entrance. Despite this formidable protection, the inner precincts of the fort were twice breached by hostile incursions. On Easter Monday, 1916, two sentries tried to relieve the monotony of pacing back and forward before the entrance by glancing sideways at a nearby football match. One of the players booted the ball in their direction. A half dozen players raced after it – and quickly overpowered the sentries. The footballers – in reality a raiding party of Irish Volunteers – disarmed the sentries, gained entry, seized what guns and ammunition they could carry, and then attempted to set fire to the remaining stocks. On their hasty departure the fire was quickly extinquished before reaching the bulk of the munitions. But the Easter Rebellion had been launched with a spectacular and morale-boosting coup – and by the end of the week 450 people were killed, 2,614 wounded, one of the finest streets in Europe destroyed, and a city centre gutted.

The second such raid occured on the 23 December 1939, almost seventeen years to the day when the Magazine Fort was handed over by the British military forces to the brand-new Irish Free State Army. The raid took place on Saturday, the night before Christmas Eve. Vigilance was lax; a festive mood prevailed. An IRA raiding party, well armed and accompanied by forty lorries, had little difficulty gaining entry. They completely took over the fort. They also took rifles, grenades and over a million rounds of ammunition. As a mere five-year old I well remember the stunned effect this had on my elders (whose attention hitherto had largely been directed towards mainland Europe and the beginnings of the Second World War, the issuing of gas masks and the imminent prospect of food rationing). It's my earliest recollection of the words 'million' and 'IRA'. I had no way of knowing then that the bulk of the Irish army's ammunition had been stolen or that a ramshackle soldiery prepared to repel every invader – German, British, Russian, Italian, American – hadn't a bullet to its name! I needn't have worried. That festive and convivial mood of which the raiding party had taken advantage – and the booze boasts that so often accompany such feats (to say nothing of the movement of a convoy of forty lorries and the concealment of such vast quantities of equipment) saw to it that not only were all the hijacked munitions recaptured before the New Year but that most of the 'boyohs' were arrested and imprisoned. But for the drinking habits of the people, the law courts would have hardly anything to do!

And, thank God, the Gestapo or the Red Army never invaded. It was probably just as well for them that they didn't. My beloved maternal grandfather Joe 'the Marine' Corrigan (or, more correctly, Private 68007 Corrigan, ever since his enlistment in the Irish army in 1923) constantly reassured his grandsons, with that confidence engendered by a few bottles of stout and a sharp penknife working deftly over his nugget of dark plug tobacco, that if any of 'them damn foreigners, be they Rooshian, English, German, Eye-talian or Yanks, either singly or together, ever attempt to set foot on any spot between Skerries and Greystones, then meself and the lads won't be long about givin' them short shrift. And ye may depend on that!' Two or three days at most, he reckoned. He did, however, in a reflective pause brought on by the first puff from his pipe, confess to some anxiety about housing upwards of ten million prisoners of war in the recently opened Curragh Detention Camp alongside the IRA 'boyohs' already inside for the Magazine Fort raid.

The Yanks, of course, did 'invade', but only at the end of the war when they came as free-spending victors and, therefore, welcomed guests. Sleek, with their crew-cut hairstyles and well-tailored uniforms, air force and naval officers on week-long furloughs thronged the Gresham, the Shelbourne, Jammet's and the Dolphin in their search for a way of living that had almost disappeared since the cataclysm of 1939, and for the steaks, salmon and cream denied to the rest of starving and war-rationed Europe. They came with their abundance of soft-packeted Chesterfield and Marlboro cigarettes and their Wrigley's chewing gum, carefully doling out one of the former or casually peeling off one of the latter as bribes to us street urchins with the question: 'Say, kid, where does a guy locate the broads in this burg?' We quickly learned their lingo, took their cigarettes for our older brothers and their silver-wrapped strips of sweet gum for our own secret delights, and learned that 'locate the broads' translated easily into 'findin' wimmen' or 'clickin' mots'. We directed the eager Yanks towards the Hollow or the main road of Phoenix Park. It mattered nothing to us how they fared afterwards. Besides, it was a well-known fact that the American forces were the best equipped in the world. In addition to flying fortresses, flack jackets and jeeps it was rumoured that they had a new gadget called a French letter.

The Magazine Fort was conveniently situated near the artillery practice ranges and the Fifteen Acres was frequently appropriated for reviews, exercises, parades and military camps. The soldierly displays appealed to the seventeen-year-old Wolfe Tone who longed to have 'a red coat and cockade, with a pair of gold epaulets', though at that age, and on his admission, the hankering for a uniform had more to do with cutting a fine figure and 'clicking mots' than dreams of martial glory. Thackeray describes such reviews:

> Here you may behold garrison races, and reviews; Lord Lieutenants in brown great coats; aides de camp scampering about like mad in blue; fat colonels roaring 'Charge' to immense heavy dragoons; dark rifle men lining woods and firing; galloping canoneers banging and blazing right and left.

In a sense the park is really all about lord lieutenants 'in brown great coats'. The Dublin historian Elrington Ball mentions a 'manor house of the Phoenix' which stood on the site of the Magazine Fort, and how this house became the summer residence of the Lord Lieutenant, or Viceroy, in 1619 and during the reign of James I. There was need for such a rural retreat in the dog days. The prevailing winds then, as now, were from the west, away from the fetid odours of the crowded town huddled about the walls of Dublin Castle and the vice-regal apartments. His Majesty's supreme representative needed a periodic escape from the summer stench of the decaying medieval town with its middens, offal, dung, refuse, ash heaps and nearby fish market. The clean air of Thomas's Hill offered the escape. The house of the Phoenix became the summer residence of the viceroys and continued to be so until it was superceded towards the end of the seventeenth century by a house in Chapelizod by the banks of the Liffey.

And then the great Viceroy Ormonde burst on the scene. His return to his native land in 1665, in the euphoria of the Stuart Restoration, was not only welcomed with a tremendous civic reception but with anticipation of his great plans for the improvement of the city. Legend has it that in London Ormonde had seen how a pretty orange-seller named Nell Gwynne – moved to tears by the common sight of old soldiers broken in the wars and reduced to begging their bread in the streets – tried to prevail on her royal paramour Charles

II to build a hospital for the old war veterans. Ormonde took the hint and soon outdid his master by building the Royal Hospital at Kilmainham for military pensioners in 1680 (a few years earlier than the better-known Chelsea Hospital in London). And thus, Ormonde's hospital for maimed war veterans – and God knows that Ireland in those days had many of them – was the first of its kind in the British Empire. It was also Ireland's first classical building and it ushered in the architectural development of Dublin.

Soon after, he purchased the 'Phoenix and adjoining Newtown Lands from Alderman Hutchinson and Christopher Fagan of Feltrim for £3,000 in order to create a royal deer park'. Before he was recalled to London in 1669 he'd already managed to suggest the ideas for the Liffey quays, St Stephen's Green, civic pride and the importance of 'keeping up the splendour of government'. Dublin owes much to his vision, sophistication and tolerance. Those qualities (300 years ago, as today) were taken advantage of by 'get-rich-quick' jerry-builders and cowboys. One of them, William Dodson, was commissioned by Ormonde to build the boundary wall enclosing the deer park (the ancestors of today's herd were imported from London at the time). Dodson's fees were exorbitant; he farmed out the work at one third the price to an even lower grade of chancers, the walls soon fell down, and the expatriate deer had great fun darting in and out through the horse traffic on Chapelizod Road. (A century later, the house which is now the American ambassador's residence was built by another chancer, Sir John de Blacquiere, a self-seeking custodian of not only the park's herds but of his own pecuniary interests who insinuated his way into the self-imposed and well-paid duties attaching to park rangership; he was quickly nicknamed the 'King's Cowboy'. I wonder if that's where the term originated?)

It would seem, too, that in addition to a royal deer enclosure Ormonde intended the park to be used by the citizens. In this regard he had to contend with his King's desire to make a present of it to one of the royal mistresses, Barbara Villiers. Ormonde resisted strenuously. Barbara pouted, scowled, raged and then hissed that she hoped to see the day when the elderly Ormonde was hanging from a gibbet. The urbane and seventy-eight-year-old duke merely smiled and said he would be content to live to see the day when the celebrated young beauty grew old. Dublin kept its park.

Other viceroys came and went: Ormonde's own grandson, Wharton, Carteret, the dukes of Bolton, Grafton, Fitzwilliam, Sackville, Rutland, Bessborough et al, most giving their names to Dublin streets, all having the burgeoning park as their pleasance. Pre-eminent among them was the Earl of Chesterfield (Lord-Lieutenant, 1744–47). Maurice Craig, in his invaluable study of the period *Dublin 1660–1860*, perfectly describes Chesterfield (or rather perfectly dismisses the long line of dreary 'deputies of deputies' with whom Chesterfield so splendidly contrasts) in the following felicitous phrase: 'He was a great exception to the usual run of beefeating, bored and bigoted English nonentities who succeeded each other in dismal and stodgy pomp at Dublin Castle.'

During a short and tactful administration Chesterfield won over the Dubliners with his charm, wit and tolerance. He possessed much of Ormonde's vision and probably surpassed him in intellectual powers and refinement. He fully appreciated the park, planted neatly arranged patterns of trees on its broad expanses, built a new road through it, and had the Phoenix Column – or the 'ould Eagle', whichever you prefer – grandly erected. His political talents were considerable and his fine manners and literary reputation fascinated his contemporaries. While the jaundiced Mitchel in his *History of Ireland* asserts that Chesterfield was sent here to woo Catholic opinion away from the lure of throwing in its lot with Bonnie Prince Charlie's Highland Rebellion of 1745, it is evident from some of Chesterfield's actions and writings (especially those letters to his son in the Hague) that he was liberal in attitude and personally favoured a relaxation of the Penal Laws and allowing Catholics to openly practice their religion. Oddly enough, the only other prominent Englishman of the period who supported the same view was a man of somewhat different character and background, Dr Samuel Johnson, who spurned Chesterfield's belated offer of patronage in his memorable letter containing the words:

> Is not a patron, my lord, one who looks with unconcern on a man struggling for life in the water, and, when he has reached ground, encumbers him with help? The notice which you have been pleased to take of my labours, had it been early, had kind; but it has been delayed till I am indifferent, and cannot enjoy it; till I am solitary, and cannot impart it*; till I am known, and do not want it. I hope it is no very cynical asperity not to confess obligations where no benefit has been received, or to be unwilling that the public should consider me as owing that to a patron which Providence has enabled me to do for myself . . . your lordship's most humble, most obedient servant, – Sam. Johnson.

As Dubliners say of the ultimate put down: 'Sure, where would you get it?'

Chesterfield, more than anyone, put the vice-regal imprimatur on the Phoenix Park. The house built in 1751 for Nathaniel Clements ('Park Ranger and Keeper of the Game') was purchased from his son thirty years later as a new summer residence for the lord-lieutenants. With wings and a north portico added in the early 1800s and dubbed the Vice-Regal Lodge, it became not only a suitable dwelling for successive viceroys but was used by George IV, Edward VII and George V during their state visits to Ireland over the next century. It is now Aras An Uachtarain, the official residence of the presidents of Ireland since 1938.

The next great viceroy was Richard Colley Wellesley (ex-Governor-General of India, later Marquis Wellesley, and eldest brother of the Duke of Wellington). Unlike his much more famous younger brother, who once deprecated his Irish birthplace with the words: 'Being born in a stable does not mean that one is a horse', Richard seems to have had a certain fondness for the 'ould Sod'. No mean soldier himself (and, for the times, a strong-minded and

* A sad reference to the death of Johnson's beloved wife, Elizabeth.

liberal gentleman), he did as much as any of his class to combat the endemic Irish scourges of bigotry and famine. Both brothers, along with many other aristocratic fornicators, were prominently mentioned as ex-lovers in Harriette Wilson's bestselling 'tell all, name names' autobiography of 1825.

At the early age of fifteen the beautiful Harriette had been launched in fashionable London as a *demi-mondaine*, or high-class call girl, by a procuress named Mrs Porter. In 1825, when Harriette had reached her fortieth birthday and was gradually running out of well-heeled paramours, she decided to publish her memoirs. It was no creative impulse or desire for literary fame that motivated her confessions; one of her many lovers, the Duke of Beaufort, had meanly defaulted on an agreed annuity of £500 for her amorous favours, instead offering a once-and-for-all lump sum of £1,200. Harriette decided it was time to nail the lot of them. Her autobiography was preceded by a publicity bombardment intended to scare potential victims into paying handsomely to keep their names out of subsequent editions. The threat worked; panic-stricken members held urgent meetings at Brooks's, White's, the Athenium and United Services clubs, all stridently declaring for a counter-offensive. A Piccadilly stonemason named Blore – whom Harriette had ridiculed in her first serialised episode for the boorish nature of his advances – was induced to take a libel action. For his trouble he was awarded £300. The notoriety surrounding the case ensured the success of the subsequent episodes. Harriette and her publisher, Stockdale, earned £10,000 within the year. The publisher had to erect barricades in front of his premises, and Harriette had sufficient royalities to live very agreeably in Paris and far away from the furore.

Alas, those readers of the time hoping for the thrill of some lurid revelation about their betters were to be disappointed. Though libellous when published, the work was never pornographic. The 644 pages of my own copy ('reprinted in full from the original edition' in 1929, and purchased for a few pence on a quayside book barrow) contains nothing more salacious than the following:

> 'My lord,' exclaimed Mrs Porter, interrupting him, 'I have had three applications this very month for the girl they call Harriette . . .' 'My good woman,' said Wellington, without making any remarks on her story, 'my time is precious. One hundred guineas are yours, and as much Harriette's, if you can induce her to give me the meeting.'

And of Richard, the older and vice-regal brother, she has only this to say:

> Wellesley's carriage drove up to my door, in less than an hour after his man had left me. His Lordship appeared the very essence of everything most *recherché*. In superfine elegance. He was, in fact, all essence! Such cambric, white as driven snow! Such embroidery! Such diamonds! Such a brilliant snuff-box! Such seals and chains! . . . It was too much, too overpowering for a poor, honest, unaffected Suissess like me . . . Wellesley took up his hat, and ran downstairs. I followed him, laughing loudly, till he got into his carriage . . .

The little 'Suissess' (Harriette's real name was Dubochet, the daughter of a Swiss clock-maker) took a few hundred more pages of the same before getting to the more famous brother:

> Wellington, who has sighed over me and groaned over me by the hour, talked of my wonderful beauty, ran after me, bribed Mrs Porter over and over again, after I refused to listen to her overtures, only for a single smile from his beautiful Harriette! Did he not kneel? And was I not the object of his first, his most ardent wishes, on his arrival from Spain?

Perhaps suspecting such interminable piffle from the amusing but empty-headed Harriette, the victor of Waterloo could easily meet the threat of her forthcoming book with his still quoted words: 'Publish and be damned!' He was shaping up for the premiership, she was a has-been. The moral influences, the rectitude, the humbug and the hypocrisy of the Victorian era were not to be long delayed. Harriette, a pious old widow, returned from Paris and died in 1846. The Wellesley brothers died around the same time. The full-blooded, high-spirited, boisterous and scandalous age was long past and buried with them. All that was left were their dusty memoirs and their cold monuments.

The great duke had his testimonial monument solidly planted in Phoenix Park, 205-feet high, its bas-reliefs depicting graphic battle scenes from Wellington's campaigns and cast in metal from captured cannon guns. But some of the citizens strolling beneath its shadow were much more inclined to look back to the battles of the Yellow Ford and Vinegar Hill for inspiration rather than Badajoz or Waterloo. Some muttered darkly and scowled at the lofty monument; it was not merely pique or annoyance at the old 'born-in-a-stable' quip, or dissatisfaction with the waste of so much public money – £22,000 to erect it in 1817! – when in the crowded tenements and hovels outside the park there was ample evidence of the cheapness of life and the dearness of everything else. Some conspired; a new and nastier form of nationalism was taking over.

Knowing that hungry and God-fearing people rarely rub their tattered shirts against naked bayonets, the Invincible conspirators saw assassination as a political expedient. The well-planned murder of some notable figure might strike fear into the powers-that-be and effect reforms without the necessity of open rebellion. It was a forlorn, misguided hope. It resulted in the brutal stabbing of Chief Secretary Lord Frederick Cavendish and Under Secretary Thomas Burke while they were casually walking through the park on a May evening in 1882. The murders profoundly shocked Irish society. There was a national shudder of horror, and even Parnell was so affected that he offered to withdraw from public life.

James Carey, town councillor and small-time building contractor, was the ringleader and the eldest of the eighteen Dublin workmen arrested for the killings. He soon turned Queen's evidence and informed on his fellow-conspirators, including James 'Skin-the-Goat' Fitzharris, the Dublin jarvey who had conveyed some of the assassins to the park in his cab and had waited nearby to assist in their escape. Five of the conspirators were hanged at Kilmainham Gaol. Fitzharris was sentenced to life imprisonment. Carey, in disguise and in disgrace and with a new identity, the Queen's pardon and the Queen's money in his pocket, was spirited away to a new life in one of Her Majesty's far-flung colonies.

As a child I remember hearing a ballad of the time known as 'Skin-the-Goat's Curse on Carey'. Some years ago I came across a copy of it, through the good offices of that great Dublin balladeer and reciter George Mullins. Here's the last stanza:

> When the equator is crossed, may the rudder be lost,
> And his vessel be wafted ashore,
> To some cannibal isle near the banks of the Nile,
> Where savages jump and roar;
> With a big sharp knife may they take his life,
> While his vessel is still afloat,
> And pick his bones as clean as stones,
> Is the prayer of poor Skin the Goat.

Carey crossed the Equator alright, but it wasn't the cannibals who got him. Travelling on the same ship to South Africa was a Donegal Invincible named Patrick O'Donnell. He shot Carey dead and in turn was hanged for his crime. Meanwhile, back in Dublin, the secret society rapidly disintegrated into a sordid and vengeful round of infighting. An innocent young man named Joe Poole (himself the unsuspecting target of a murder gang) was hanged for the shooting of John Kenny near the latter's home in Seville Place. The only evidence against Poole was that of his own brother-in-law, Lamie, who 'according to his own testimony was steeped to the lips in infamy and crime', as one Dublin paper put it at the time. With a dozen needless and tragic deaths, all the Invincibles had succeeded in doing was to create by an inevitable process the informers and their victims, figures that play so deplorable and so prominent a part in that bloodstained and miserable chapter.

On his release from prison in the early years of this century, and in poor health, Fitzharris obtained employment for a time as a Corporation watchman, or 'gotchy', in the East Wall area (largely through the efforts of William T. Cosgrave, then a Sinn Fein councillor), and he died some time before the 1916

Rebellion. About ten years ago his granddaughter informed me that even on his deathbed he refused to divulge the name of the assasin to members of his own family; with what were virtually his last words he closed the chapter on the Phoenix Park Murders and the Invincibles with the statement: 'I've kept this secret for so long, and I've suffered for it, that it's best now if I take it to the grave with me.'

'Skin-the-Goat' was only a confused, still-lingering legend when we were children – a kind of Jack Frost, banshee or bogeyman figure lurking in the tribal folklore or somewhere out there in the misty shadows of the Fifteen Acres; he might just appear if we hadn't finished gathering chestnuts by dusk.

In those days the park was only about chestnuts, snowballs, monkeys and lions in the zoo. And it was ever a repository of Dublin wit. It is difficult for me to pass the Dog Pond or the People's Pond on a winter's morning and not remember the words of a spread-eagled skater on the ice calling out: 'Why the hell is it that when water freezes the feckin' slippery side is always uppermost?' – or to pass the Hollow and not recall a story told to me many years ago of an elderly soprano on the bandstand, and with the backing of a string ensemble, entertaining the crowd with a spirited rendition of an old Victorian drawing-room favourite entitled 'I'll Hang My Harp on a Willow Tree'. Each time she attempted the high note she faltered and quavered. Repeatedly she made a stab at 'I'll hang my harp on a willow tree-ee' – until a listener called out, 'Ma'am, try hangin' it on a lower branch!' The park is full of such echoes.

And if the world of Ormonde and Chesterfield is long dead, those of us who find an exquisite pleasure in the flavour of an epoch cannot do better, in order to appreciate something of the period in which such worthies flourished, than to walk or cycle through the Phoenix Park. In its broad acres we may imagine, almost gaze upon, the stout figure of Ormonde, the blue-frocked coat of Chesterfield and the hook-nosed Wellesleys reviewing their battalions of dragoons and riflemen. Or with reverence we may look upon the grassy plot where a Chief Secretary in yellow gloves and side whiskers and an Under Secretary who refused to carry a revolver, and who said, 'If they want to get me they can', together met their death.

And with Sheridan Le Fanu we can gaze back at the vanished pomp and dignity of the vice-regal era as one Lord Lieutenant after another climbed 'into his emblazoned coach and six, with hanging footmen, as wonderful as Cinderella's, and out-riders outblazing the liveries of the troops, and rolling grandly away in sunshine and dust . . .'

OPEN

· 6 ·

The Liberties

APART from an occasional Sunday morning visit to the bird market in Bride Street as children, we rarely visited that area of the city known as the Liberties. The locality in those days didn't make an immediate appeal. The full charm of the Liberties and of its inhabitants is revealed only after long acquaintance. Well into the 1950s as soon as one left the main thoroughfares and the itineraries of the Castle, Christchurch and St Patrick's Cathedral, one frequently found oneself in what seemed a very pleasureless world. The purely picturesque aspect of some of the last remaining triangular gabled houses was quickly exhausted by the squalor of ancient and over-crowded tenements, banners of washing hung out to dry across narrow laneways, the combined smell of piggeries, cattle yards, stale ullage, and the all-pervading miasma of melting mules and boiling glue of horse hides, bones and animal carcasses from Keefe's, the knackers. One circled the place like a hunter's dog, though, unlike the dog, trying not to sniff the air.

The once distinctive curvilinear gables of the houses – commonly called Dutch Billys, as they dated from around the time of the reign of William of Orange – may well have been influenced by the Great Fire of London in 1666. That terrible blaze raged for four days and destroyed 13,000 houses and ninety churches. Fortunately, fewer than half a dozen people lost their lives. One good result of the fire was that dwellings of timber and thatch gave way to brick and stone, and there was a determined effort to broaden the streets. Dublin's Dutch Billys were probably a development of earlier 'fire hazard' timber-framed gabled houses translated into brick and slate and surviving much longer in the Liberties than elsewhere in the city because the decline in the locality's once-flourishing weaving industries of the eighteenth century meant a disincentive to developing the area.

The spirit of survival has always existed in the Liberties. Sometimes the old wrinkled faces seen in the Coombe, Pimlico, Meath Street and Francis Street may betray the experience of hard times, but rarely do they contain the stigma of meanness, mediocrity or defeat. And only they – representatives of that sadly, slowly dwindling generation – tried by the rigours of their existence, can properly describe with the necessary force and colour the harsh living conditions, the needs and the hopes of 'the ould days'. For the Liberties means more than a mere topographical location. Its inhabitants regard themselves as more than ordinary citizens. They are the 'rale' Dubliners, squarely placed in the oldest part of the town, custodians of old traditions, speech patterns, witticisms, whimsical lore and bawdy ballads. Authenticity is the keynote here.

The Liberties, I sometimes think, is as much a state of mind as an enclave within the greater city. Its restless, clamorous history has made it such. The district takes its name from the small medieval ecclesiastical liberties of St Patrick's, Christchurch, St Sepulchre's and the larger liberty of St Thomas's Abbey, which since 1210 were exempt from the jurisdiction of the mayor of the city. The successive abbots and prelates had full authority in their respective domains. They controlled weights and measures for bread, brewing, taxes, markets, and had temporal as well as spiritual jurisdiction, with the power to imprison wrong-doers, set up pillories and execute criminals.

With the Reformation the monks were sent packing and the abbey and lands of St Thomas were granted to William Brabazon, under-treasurer to Henry VIII. Brabazon's grandson became Earl of Meath in 1627, around the time the last of the old monastic buildings were torn down, and his Dublin estate of Thomas Court and Donore (still retaining exemption from city jurisdiction) thereafter became known as the Earl of Meath's Liberties. Until an Act of Parliament of 1859 abolished all such anachronistic institutions, the Liberties had its own manor courthouse presided over by a seneschal with legal powers almost on a par with those of Dublin's lord mayor.

It was to this 'town within a town' – almost medieval in character, so congested that the houses were made taller – that immigrant linen and silk workers (French Huguenots, Dutch and Flemish Protestants) flocked after the Revocation of the Edict of Nantes in 1685. This influx of foreign craftsmen and workers with their families further added to the distinctive nature of the Liberties and its people. Economic forces put the finishing touches to that sense of separateness. After the boom years of the early eighteenth century the mercantile centre of Dublin was wrenched downriver to the environs of Gandon's new Custom House. The shift coincided with a glut of foreign silks and fabrics on the Dublin market and a British embargo and duties on exports abroad of Irish woolen and linen products. The weavers were ruined. The Liberties became something of a backwater. Fashionable, residential and commercial Dublin spread eastward, then north east for a while, then south east and, after the Act of Union, increasingly in the latter direction. Georgian Dublin was the work of aristocrats, proud in their memory of illustrious forerunners, and of the parvenu, the wealthy merchant and the professional man anxious to emulate his 'betters' and establish his dynasty. It was always of a certain 'upper crust' complexion and never a reflection of that plebeian citizenry who were overawed by the habitations of their masters and subjugated by the majesty of Dublin Castle. The Victorian Dubliner, sprung from a race in whom the industrial spirit was crushed out by legislation and the Act of Union, failed as a manufacturer. Extreme poverty, over-crowding, starvation and neglect were among the distinguishing features of the Liberties throughout the nineteenth century and beyond.

And Liberties folk suspect they've inherited a number of qualities which mark them off from the 'ordinary' citizens. Again, their history assures them of it. It's not a form of inverted snobbery. They know they are fighters, survivors to whom personal loyalty is a tradition and a matter of honour, and they are great organisers – often on the flimsiest pretext – of convivial celebrations and hooleys. Their yarns and ballads (and the accumulated homespun wisdom of past associations that so easily blend with the living present) tell of the penury of their ancestors, the riots and ructions, and the humour that relieved lives that might otherwise have been unenduringly grim.

> Ye tradesmen all, I pray, draw near, that lives in Dublin
> town,
> A doleful story you shall hear since the weaving is pull'd
> down;
> I am a weaver by my trade in Dublin, it is known full
> well,
> Which makes my very heart to bleed for to think of our
> downfall . . .
>
> Ye weavers all, be not so sad nor do not so lament,
> For the Rev'rend Dean will you relieve at the next
> parliament,
> The Indian silks and calicoes from coming over the
> main –
> And then, brave boys, ye need not fear but the trade will
> flourish again!

Often the ballads show neither discretion nor restraint. On the introduction to Dublin of the horse-tram omnibus in 1872, a popular ballad of the day reveals a nudge-and-wink sexual imagery:

> I cocked up my finger and the car quickly stopped,
> I had not long been standing there when inside I did pop,
> I scarcely had got time when I heard the lady say
> That it's jolly to be riding on the new tramway.
>
> Riding on the tramway, that's the game for me,
> Riding on the tramway, so happy I would be;
> A noble sum of threepence is all we have to pay
> For to do the hurdy-gurdy on the new tramway!

It is through the old street ballads that we sometimes enter – as though through a rickety, ancient postern – that Dublin which now scarcely exists, and yet shabby traces of which abound everywhere. It is a Dublin which was ignorant, poor, violent, fun-loving, maudlin, melodramatic – perhaps even sordid, bawdy and banal – but, nevertheless, authentic. Much of that authenticity still lingers in the shadow of the Castle, Christchurch, St Patrick's and Taylor's Hall and around the traders' stalls in Thomas Street and the shops of Meath and Francis streets. Nowadays, when I visit the Liberties, it is usually to meet up with such great balladeers and traditional reciters as George Mullins, Frank Hart, Luke Cheevers, Paul O'Brien, Barry Gleason and their legion of blink-a-blonk, banjo-plucking, bodhran-tapping, tin-whistling and guitar-strumming colleagues. Between them they have a vast repertoire of ballads, parodies and 'rec-im-itations' – 'Knocking Nelly', 'The Maid from Cabra West', 'The Bandy-legged Barmaid', 'The Inchicore Wake', 'The Red Knickers', 'Goldilocks and the Three Teddy-Boys', 'The Ale-Wife and the Sea Crab', 'The Twang-Man' and so many more.

It has been said somewhere of such plebeian ballads and 'pomes' that they are often more direct, more realistic, and more acutely aware of their social environment than the esoteric or literary verse of true poetry; that they have the waspish sting of irony and the bludgeon of bawdiness that scatters pomposity and 'preciousness'. They are the songs of a people who, no matter how poor, always had something good to look at and lampoon – if not Georgian buildings, Stephen's Green, or grandees in Phoenix Park, then at least the constant street pageantry of huxters' shops, hawkers, buskers, three-card tricksters and those charlatans who traded on the incredulity of the luckless among the throng.

And along with the ballads and recitations are the still-remembered and still-repeated tales of epic 'come-uppances', like the time Queen Victoria on her final state visit to Dublin in April 1900 grandly and curiously enquired the price of eggs from a curtseying stall-holder on Thomas Street:

> 'A quid for a dozen eggs?' sez the oul Queen, in a prefermosity of amazement. 'Begorrah, eggs must be very scarce in Dublin!' 'Nor-at-all,' sez the dealer-woman. 'Eggs is plentiful – but monarchs is scarce, thanks be ta Jaysus!'

There is an apocryphal echo of the same attitude in the yarn of the old shawlie with her time-battered jug hobbling into a dairy in the Coombe during the bovine foot-and-mouth epidemic of the 1940s and, for the fifth day running, being told by the dairyman that there was no fresh milk to be had

– all he could offer her was a tiny tin of condensed milk. 'I suppose it'll have to do', she muttered disconsolately before adding: 'We'll all be bollixed for sure if them condensed cows die of that feckin' foot-an'-mou' as well!'

And there's even a yarn – it matters little that it's probably untrue – that some virtuoso of the ilk of Paganini or Handel (perhaps triumphantly returning from the Fishamble Street Theatre just down the hill after the world premiere of his *Messiah*?) continued to play his violin to the rapturous crowd of admiring well-wishers in the street. At a particularly *pianissimo* passage an irate tenement-dweller leaned out of an upstairs window and bellowed: 'Shag off! One scraper at the door is enough!' (A reference, of course, to the fact that most Georgian houses had a metal shoe-scraper embedded in the stone of the top step outside the halldoor for the removal of street mud and dung before entering; many of these scrapers still exist and are highly valued by house-owners and collectors.)

As I said, it matters not whether a tale is true in all particulars. What really matters in places like the Liberties is that the tale is still worthy of repetition (with or without embellishments) and that the past must easily blend with the present. This is understandable when one realises that the area is the repository of the remaining vestiges of medieval Dublin – the Castle, Christchurch, St Patrick's, St Audeon's (and, below it, the ancient citadel's remaining fortified wall) – and that Liberties folk, not all of them too sure of the history or provenance of such buildings, are nonetheless proud of the fact that such edifices have always stood guardian over their ancestors' homes and workplaces.

The castle, for instance, is a microcosm of Dublin's and Ireland's history. 'You are to erect a castle at Dublin in such suitable place as you shall judge most expedient, as well to curb the city as to defend it, if occasion shall require', wrote King Henry II in 1205 to his Lord Judiciary of Ireland, Meiller Fitz-Henry. The new Norman overlords needed such castles to awe their recently acquired vassals and to curb incipient revolt. Dublin Castle was frequently under attack from the marauding clansmen of the O'Byrne and the O'Toole sweeping down from the the Wicklow and

Dublin mountains. It also endured a fierce siege by the forces of the Scottish invader Edward de Bruce in 1316, and fifty years later, Lionel, Duke of Clarence, newly appointed King's Lieutenant, had to rebuild the entire castle and strongly fortify the town. Throughout its long and turbulent history the grim fortress was the background to some of the darkest scenes in Irish history – massacres, executions, trial by ordeal, imprisonments – as well as the setting for some of its most glittering events.

It was not until Elizabeth's time that it became the residence of the Viceroy and not until Chesterfield's term of office (1744–47), and under his careful and aesthetic eye, that it began to take on the appearance that it has today. The main quadrangle was built in the early Georgian era. In 1752 the handsome clock-tower in the Upper Yard, together with the stone gateways on either side, were erected. The leaden statues of Justice and Fortitude surmounting the gates were the work of Van Nost, then the leading sculptor in Ireland. And it must have been one of the leading political lampooners who added the popular slogan:

> Statue of Justice, mark well her station,
> Her face to the Castle, her back to the Nation!

It was at this period, and particularly in the aftermath of the 1798 Rebellion, that the odium so long associated with Castle rule among the masses is first noted. 'There is no Irish hen-wife,' Arthur Griffith once remarked, 'who believes that good Irishmen can ever be hatched in the Dublin Castle incubator.'

It was only one class of the populace who saw the Castle as a venue for masquerades, musical recitals and amateur theatricals. The zenith of entertaining was reached during the period of Lord Carlisle's viceroyalty. Writing to her friend Lady Louisa Stuart in London in April 1782, Miss Herbert could enthuse: 'We outdo you in dissipation! Nothing can be so gay as Dublin is . . . the Castle twice a week, the opera twice a week, with plays, assemblies and suppers to fill the time.' Great festivities marked the inauguration of the Order of St Patrick in 1783 and with it the commencement of the 'Dublin season'. It was George IV (who held court at Dublin Castle during his visit of 1821) who began the custom of kissing young ladies and debutantes on their first presentation. That pleasant custom – pleasant, perhaps, for the portly and elderly viceroys, if not always so for the nervous young ladies – was maintained until the early years of this century by successive lord lieutenants.

One of the great 'kissers' was Wellington's brother, the Marquess of Wellesley, who twice filled the office of Lord Lieutenant. His earlier service in India seems to have imbued him with ideas of oriental splendour, which his own moderate means could not easily maintain. He was twice married to a 'fortune', his second wife being an American widow, Mary Patterson, who, by the irony of life, was connected through marriage with the family of Napoleon, Wellington's old battlefield adversary. In 1826, writing to a friend in America, Madame Bonaparte gave the following account of Mrs Patterson's marriage to the Lord Lieutenant:

> I suppose you have all heard of Mary's great good fortune in marrying the Marquess of Wellesley. He is 66 years old; so much in debt that the plate on his table is hired; had his carriage once seized in the streets of Dublin; and has a great part of his salary mortgaged. But with all these drawbacks he is considered a very great match, owing to his rank.

With the Victorian era music became much in vogue at the Castle – harpers, Moore's melodies, the airs of Balfe and Wallace, and visiting celebrities like Grisi and Malibran delighting the opera-lovers. The term of the Earl of Cadogan (1895–1900) marks the last of the great viceroys and of Castle entertainments on the grand scale. The new century brought changes; the political climate suggested a diminution of grandeur. And there was scandal – in July 1907 the Crown Jewels in Dublin Castle were stolen just prior to the state visit of Edward VII. Valued at the then figure of £50,000, these were in the custody of Sir Arthur Vicars, the Ulster King of Arms; but despite the combined efforts of some of Europe's best detectives and the holding of a sworn enquiry into the circumstances of the theft, mystery still surrounds the disappearance of the jewels and the whereabouts of the booty to this day.

The First World War caused the eclipse of Castle festivities, with the State Apartments being fitted up as a hospital; and the subsequent Irish War of Independence saw the eclipse of the Castle as the focal point of British rule in Ireland. While it successfully repulsed an attack by insurgents during the Easter Rebellion of 1916, the Castle was quietly handed over to the new Irish State less than six years later. In January 1922 the last of a long line of viceroys, Lord Fitzalan, formally surrendered the Castle to Michael Collins (the newly appointed Chairman of the Irish Government, and as such the chief officer concerned in taking over of the administration from the British) when the latter proudly marched into the brocade-hung Council Chamber and produced a copy of the recently signed and ratified Anglo-Irish Treaty. It was only the second time Collins had visited the Castle. Two years before, with a price on his head and disguised as a sooty-faced helper on a coal cart, he penetrated the defensive cordon to make contact with his agents inside. 'That was the time that we planned our counter-intelligence system in the Holy-of-Holies itself', he later said. Thus, after more than 700 years, Meiller Fitz-Henry's 'stronge fosses and walls . . . as well to curb the city as to defend it' were finally breached – not from without, but from within.

Those early Norman invaders were also into the business of erecting great cathedrals and abbeys as a means of appeasing the Almighty for their bloody conquests. If the Castle is a microcosm of Ireland's history, then as much, or more, could be written about St Patrick's and its famous dean, or Christchurch, or St Catherine's (now, alas, derelict) outside the portals of which the romantic young rebel Emmet was executed, or St Werburgh's (which had its spire removed after Emmet's abortive rising of 1803 for fear that, as it overlooked the courtyard of Dublin Castle, it might be used by snipers or assassins).

Like so many things in Ireland's checkered history, Dublin's two proud cathedrals, Christchurch and St Patrick's, owe their existence to a quarrel as much as to piety. Christchurch, the older of the two, was first a wooden structure built around 1039 by King Sitric Silkenbeard, one of the first christianised Norse-Dubliners. One hundred and forty years later it was rebuilt in stone, and in larger dimensions, by a Norman adventurer at the behest of a saintly bishop. Richard de Clare, or Strongbow, the doughty leader of those Anglo-Norman conquerors, was laid to rest there; his stone-hewn effigy is still pointed out to visitors to the cathedral he had helped to build. The heart of St Laurence O'Toole, Archbishop and Patron of Dublin, is encased in an iron receptacle in a little chapel to the right of the high altar. He had urged the building of the cathedral. Today it stands as a kind of memorial to both of them, a soldier of fortune and a saintly but shrewd negotiator – a disparate duo that were to have many mental descendants in Dublin's subsequent history. The surprisingly large crypt of Christchurch – containing among its many relics the ancient stocks for malefactors and the city's oldest secular statues (believed to be those of Charles II and James II) – was built at the time of Strongbow and St Laurence and is Dublin's oldest surviving building.

One of St Laurence O'Toole's successors, Archbishop John Comyn – chafing at the continued interference of city officials – quit Christchurch in 1192, moved his episcopal jurisdiction outside the city walls, took over a little wooden church on a marshy island (where, tradition has it, St Patrick converted his first batch of Poddle-side pagans) and set up his own collegiate church. Comyn's immediate successor, Henry de Loundres (perhaps as a *quid pro quo* or as a reward for undertaking to build a bigger and better defensive castle at Dublin) was allowed to raise Comyn's collegiate church to the status of cathedral and to designate its immediate environs as the liberty of St Sepulchre. His adherents claimed that, while technically speaking the stone-built Christchurch might be older than their newly built St Patrick's Cathedral, each were built on the site of older wooden churches – of which St Patrick's was unarguably the more ancient and therefore should be the primary institution. The opposing faction of clerics at Christchurch vehemently disputed this. The rivalry – often bitter and heated and with secular interests taking sides – continued for almost a century until a conference in 1300 decided in favour of Christchurch. It was agreed that it had the precedence of age and henceforth should be the site for the consecration of all future archbishops of Dublin.

Before, during and after the Reformation the centrally located Christchurch enjoyed the patronage of the Castle officials and the more important citizens. It might have eventually eclipsed the influence of St Patrick's but for the incumbency of Jonathan Swift as Dean from 1713 to 1745. Words spoken from his pulpit (it can still be seen there) and more especially words penned by his hand in the candle-glow of his deanery, have reached the earth's remotest corners. Whether an ideal clergyman or not, whether thoroughly orthodox in his theological opinions – Queen Anne could never forget that his *A Tale of a Tub*, which she considered vulgar and offensive, brought religion into ridicule! – Swift, from his pulpit, poured forth his genuine and deep compassion for the oppressed and revealed savage satisfaction in exposing the tyranny and brutal insolence of the oppressors. 'To expose vice, and to make people laugh with innocence', he wrote, 'does more public service than all the Ministers of State. . . . If I ridicule the follies and corruptions of a court, a ministry, or a senate, are they not amply paid by pensions, titles, and power, while I expect no other reward than that of laughing with a few friends in a corner.'

He came back to Ireland expecting to die, as he complained, 'like a poisoned rat in a hole'. But his relationship with his native soil, and with a native population that he despised, underwent a strange revolution. Those who had neither the energy, the will nor the wit to protect their own interest, and therefore could hardly grumble if they were deprived of them, soon had a brilliant and stentorian voice lambasting all and sundry on their behalf. His political tracts in their cause, *The Drapier Letters* and, to a lesser extent, *Gulliver's Travels* allowed him to wield immense power, which 'all the circumstances considered, is probably without parallel in the history of English politics' (Cecil A. Moore, *English Prose of the Eighteenth Century*, New York: Henry Holt & Co., 1934). 'He held no political appointment, he received, as he boasted, not a penny of salary; yet his patrons were well aware that the tenure of their control depended to a large extent upon his defense of their policies.' Through Swift's writings, a commonwealth of scathing wit, satire, scatology and savage excoriation of political corruption and the grosser foibles of the human race was born on the marshy isle beside the Poddle; it circled the globe and made St Patrick's more famous and historically more important than its sister cathedral of Christchurch.

The ghost of Dean Swift – his blistering invective, the charm of his letters to Stella, the passionate concern for the oppressed, his vulgarity, his satirical wit – still haunts the Liberties. He gave hundreds of pithy, colourful phrases to the language, much of which he gathered in the dingy streets and lanes clustered about his cathedral and garnered from the Dublin chatter that he loved to listen to. The reflective and observant visitor who nowadays haunts the Liberties long enough to understand its special atmosphere will see and hear evidence of this. Here, on the streets, in the pubs, the little shops and market places – thankfully the area hasn't yet succumbed to such alien importations as shopping malls – there is little masking of feelings, no use for pretension, no hint of repression, but a kind of bravura performance of humanity's common lot. Love, anger, grief, song, friendship, happiness, gossip seem more vividly revealed, more colourfully expressed than elsewhere in the city. The locality's rows of red-brick single-storey artisan dwellings suggest cobblestones, clogs, cloth caps and shawls and the racey banter and ballads that go with them. It is a place where the past is everything and the future less than nothing. We look for ghosts in the distant bygone and find them hale and hearty all about us.

The Dean would love it still. And almost anywhere within the shadow of the two cathedrals one can find a place for 'laughing with a few friends in a corner'.

· 7 ·

Howth

In a wide arc to the south of County Dublin a ring of mountains (or high foothills, if you prefer) rise above the still-spreading, still-climbing suburbs of Cabinteely, Stepaside, Sandyford, Firhouse, Old Bawn and Jobstown. Beyond these hills is County Wicklow of the wine-dark heather, the forestry plantations, the lakes, tarns and lonely moorlands of true mountain country. The two counties, Dublin and Wicklow, merge and twist and lock into each other in a semi-wilderness where the hardy hiker must climb to wind-swept summits, descend into valleys, cross streams and skirt the shoulders of other distant hills. Here and there he or she will come across a few steep acres of soggy grass confined within old and painfully built chest-high walls erected to hem in mountainy sheep and cattle. Over most of these hills and mountains lies the grandeur and the loneliness of the past. And the same hills, making a wonderful backdrop to an ancient town, can be seen from any part of Dublin.

With one notable exception the northside panorama has nothing to compare it with. Yet from almost any height in the city, look northwards and there's Howth Head, at once a promontory and a peninsula, apparently remote and even mysterious, its 576-foot summit proud against the sky. From time immemorial that summit has been a kind of barometer for the inland dwellers on the flat and fertile plains of Fingal; there is an old north county proverb which says: 'If Howth has a black cap, then Fingal may look out.' And from the dawn of history (indeed, it could be argued, until the coming of the railway in 1847) Howth enjoyed comparative isolation from the rest of the county and certainly from the mainstream of Dublin life; the old Howth family names of Rickard, Thunder, Harford, Tallon and Sweetmen are all of Norse origin and are another clue to this near isolation. For centuries the locals rarely visited the city and even then much preferred a boat journey across the bay rather than a costly, arduous and sometimes perilous land trip. The latter mode of travel invariably meant running the gauntlet of Mud Island (now Ballybough/North Strand), a notorious haunt of footpads, beggars and smugglers, or the highwaymen of Robbers Row (now Seafield Road, Dollymount), who more than once held up the Howth mail coach. And here it is interesting to note that an outbreak of cholera at Howth in 1831 (said to have been brought into the little port by a ship from China) was solely confined to that area and caused hardly a ripple of concern in the capital less than a dozen miles away. The fact illustrates both the relative isolation of the peninsula and the seemingly contradictory fact that from Norman times, and prior to the development of Dublin port in the eighteenth century, Howth Harbour was an important place of arrival and departure by sea between Ireland and Britain.

Even in my childhood and youth Howth was almost lost to the rest of County Dublin in its magnificent obsession with boats and fishing. At the mere hoisting of sail or the chug-chug of a herring boat, old men left pipes unlit and edged to the quayside, women wandered to their windows that looked down on the harbour and publicans hesitated over the topping up of creamy pints: 'Who's comin' in?' 'Is that the *Evora* puttin' out to sea?' The salty tang of seafarings and sailor talk will always be part of Howth. And the names are almost too good to be true: Doldrum Bay, Earl's Cliff, Gaskin's Leap, Fox Hole, Piper's Gut, Casana Rock, Black Jack's Well, the Bloody Stream, Nose of Howth and Puck's Rock (where, legend has it, St Nessan flung his Bible at the devil and the good book sliced right down through the cliff, severing the rock from the mainland and leaving Old Nick marooned).

There is magic in such names, the stuff of the *Hispaniola* and *Treasure Island*, lurking echoes of ancient druids, old pirates, shipwrecks, the clash of cutlass and all the history of a vanished age. And whenever Mary and I walk about this haunted headland – for haunted it surely is, and now fortunately protected by strict development-control policy from the excesses of indiscriminate concrete and brick – we take the cliff walk, or the right-of-way foot track that leads from Carrickbrack Road up through the ferns to the Ben of Howth. It is then that I cannot but recall my first-ever visit to those ancient heights.

I was a mere five- or six-year old. It was a day of high adventure, starting with a long walk from our home in Donnycarney across a country lane skirting farmland and fields (some of which were already displaying those little slats of wood and trench marks that presage future housing development) to the railway station at Killester. And, as steam 'puffing billies' were the norm, we were being treated to the novelty of a trip on the new-fangled Drum Battery train. Designed by Trinity College's Dr James Drum in 1932, four units of this battery-operated locomotive were pressed into service at the outbreak of the Second World War and were destined to play a major role in maintaining a suburban rail service throughout the fuel-shortage years of 'the Emergency'.

At Howth, after milk and biscuits and hot homemade bread in Aunt Lily's, Uncle Peter Quirke took us out in his boat round the harbour. I think the plan was to head over to Ireland's Eye, but it was soon abandoned in deference to my terror of the open sea in such a small craft. I was convinced that the trickles of bilge water slopping about my sandals indicated a leak. We put-put-putted under the towering prows of the trawlers, from the west pier to the east, while I anxiously implored everyone to observe the steadily rising water at our feet and to head back to dry land. My tearful entreaties won the day.

I was much relieved to be back on *terra firma* and almost indescribably happy when my cousins Tony, Joan and Olive brought me for a long walk through a shoulder-high wonderland of golden gorse and purple bell heather. On a hill crest they showed me an ancient cairn; they each placed a stone on it, said I must do the same and hinted at the ghost of a dead king. After my recent delivery from a watery grave, and with the sunlight of an August evening casting those strange shadows that are only known to wayfarers on a lonely Irish mountainside, I was only too happy to oblige and I wrestled the largest stone I could manage to the top of the cairn. And to this day I can still hear the faraway bleating of sheep and the barking of a wise dog and the whistle of the wind coming in from the sea. Cousin Tony, hardly a year older than myself, was not only calmly in control but knew every downward step of the track flinging itself round the shoulder of little hillocks and curving and twisting among the boggy tussocks. The girls were plucking wild blossoms and laughing every now and then. There was still a lot of daylight about, but the twinkling of house lights below in the Haggard was reassuring, nonetheless. Behind us, on the upper slopes, the ferns rustled furtively, like the whisperings of some long-ago and long-dead king.

The cairn to which my gentle cousins brought me more than fifty years ago must surely have been that one in the valley between Sheilmartin and Dun Hill, which tradition says is the burial place of Criomthain, the first Gaelic king of the locality. The Annals of the Four Masters give the date of Criomthain's death as the year 9 AD, shortly after returning from one of his piratical raids on Roman Britain, his boats laden down with captured booty and slaves. His *dun*, or fortress, is said to have been on the site of the present Baily Lighthouse, from which same eminence his womenfolk watched out for his return from sea forays and land pillage with such treasures as 'wonderful jewels, among which were a golden chariot, and a golden chess-board (inlaid) with a hundred transparent gems, and a beautiful cloak embroidered with gold'.

On another occasion Tony showed me mute but dramatic evidence of yet another kingly connection with Howth, the imprint of two feet on a stone at the West Pier. Whose were they? How had they been impressed into the hard stone? We were none too sure who George IV was, save that he was an English king who had landed in Ireland at this very spot. His footprints were marked out, and later a stone-mason named Campbell carefully incised and chiselled out the impression. The wonder of it all is that the royal feet remained steady for long enough to take an accurate marking, for on the afternoon of 9 August 1821, when George IV arrived in Howth, he was speechlessly and staggeringly drunk. And he continued in that fashion for the remainder of his month-long stay. Struggling through asthma, gout, corpulence, dissipation, drunkenness and the 'distressing looseness' of diarrhoea, His Majesty had to have a specially constructed outsize mobile lavatory on hand for his visit to the Curragh races. A Mr Massey Dawson, MP for Clonmel, and of much the same girth as the king, obligingly submitted to being measured for the royal bog-house, or 'sanitary engine' as it was called.

The drunken junket continued, and not even the death of his wife Queen Caroline could lure the jaded voluptuary back to England for her funeral. This was probably just as well. The London mob might have pelted his hypocritical mourning coach with rotten fruit, or worse. His callous ill-treatment of his wife and daughter and his numerous infidelities (even more than his squandering and his drunken behaviour) offended English sensibilities even in those boisterous times. In reality, George IV's state visit to Ireland was greatly encouraged by the government, who wanted him off the scene at the time of the queen's illness. His ministers feared violent reaction in sympathy with the long-suffering wife. George's vows of fidelity may have been less memorable to him from the fact of his having reeled into chapel to be married and having belched and hiccuped out the same vows.

The first English king to visit Ireland on a peaceful mission was also the last king of England who, habitually, succeeded in having his own pampered way in all things. And his 'peaceful mission' left an aftermath of dissension. He had arrived characteristically and unexpectedly at Howth – while the Lord Lieutenant, the members of Dublin Corporation, the gentry and an estimated 200,000 well-wishers, with bands, pavilions, flags and buntings, were assembled at Dun Laoghaire across the bay. When he didn't show up the Dun Laoghairites were chagrined, having once more lost out to their northside rivals. Then, on his departure, and with the northsiders gleefully expecting another gala day at Howth, the king opted for Dun Laoghaire, pausing just long enough and with sufficient sobriety to mitigate the earlier slight to the red-faced civic dignitaries by grandly allowing them to rechristen their pretty little township 'Kingstown'. They thankfully erected the George IV Testimonial Obelisk beside their harbour. Thackeray later described it as 'hideous . . . an obelisk stuck on four fat balls and surmounted with a crown on a cushion (the latter were not bad emblems, perhaps, of the Monarch in whose honour they were raised)'. And on Howth's West Pier the footprints are not an inappropriate memorial to a king whose only worthwhile feat was to design an army uniform and to invent a fashionable new shoe-buckle.

The then rivalry between the two harbours goes back to 1805, when it was first decided to bring the Irish mail through Holyhead to either Howth or Dun Laoghaire. A fierce controversy developed between the champions of the competing ports. Each had brand-new and extensive harbours built, each lobbied the Lord Lieutenant, the Admiralty, the Postmaster General and any other influential official or politician they could find. Howth won the first round and in August 1818 became the mail station for Dublin. By 1822, when steam-packet boats took over from sailing ships, the voyage from Holyhead was reduced from an average of fifteen hours to less than half that time. *Leigh's Road-Book of Ireland, 1832* describes Howth as:

> ... an improving port and post town of the county of Dublin, romantically situated on the promontory known by the appellation of the Hill of Howth, the highest point of which is 567 feet above high-water mark. Here the mails and passengers are landed from Holyhead without passing the bar of Dublin Bay; and Howth Harbour is the station of the Steam-Packets commanded by Officers of the Royal Navy. These vessels can leave the harbour at any time, and generally arrive at Holyhead in seven hours.

Everything seemed fine. Alas, within two years of Leigh's description, the larger design of the new packet boats and the gradual silting up of the port meant that the vessels with their Royal Navy personnel could neither leave nor enter the harbour at will. The Postmaster General quickly decided to abandon Howth and to make Kingstown-Dun Laoghaire the new station for all packets. After the first flush of success Howth lost out and within twenty years of acquiring a brand-new harbour the 'improving port and post town' had reverted to what it had always been, a pleasant fishing village. Happily, it still more or less retains that character to this day, a little town of uneven houses climbing up from the harbour's edge to enfold an ancient abbey ruin.

Scholarly authorities may differ over the age of the abbey (or Collegiate Church, as it is sometimes called), though the earliest portions are attributed to the Norse king of Dublin, Sitric, in 1042. But its shattered nave and broken aisles are a vivid reminder that Howth is one of the last bastions of that strange compromise between past and present, urban and rural, fairy tale and battlefield, with which Dublin's periphery was studded in my boyhood. It is a well-preserved ruin. I have sat on a stone under its embattled walls and have been told the story of how the fifteenth-century altar tomb of Christopher St Lawrence, Lord of Howth, was unceremoniously used by later smugglers to hide their booty, and I've dutifully murmured a hasty prayer over one of the most unusual and most poignant 'gravestones' in Ireland: two pieces of grooved tram rail erected on 'Stranger's Bank' by his mates to commemorate an unknown English track-layer who died during the influenza epidemic of 1918. It is still referred to as the 'tomb of the unknown tram-man'. Or perhaps that sense of poignancy, sadness, loss – call it what you will – has as much to do with the demise of the Howth tram as with the lonely death of an unnamed tram worker seventy-five years ago. He was well before my time – but I remember the loss of the tram.

In recent years a number of excellent books have appeared recalling the intellectual, literary and artistic *milieu* of the 1950s: the regular meetings in the Pearl Bar, McDaid's, the Palace, Mooney's at Baggot Street Bridge, and the stimulating conversations of such luminaries as Myles na gCopaleen, Paddy Kavanagh, Brendan Behan, Harry Kernoff and Larry Morrow et al. The artist and photographer Nevill Johnson says that some of them 'drifted in a whirlpool of lost endeavour, some drowned'. For others, like author James Plunkett, the 1950s 'wore a grey, tired face . . . deserted, windraked streets, bus stops cowering under the rain'. For many of us who were either too young, too shy, too 'thick', or lacking the wherewithal to hang about on the fringes of such exalted company, the 1950s meant something else. It was ushered in with the discontinuance of the city trams, the 'mortal sin' of Lenten dances, the disbandment of the Presidential Blue Hussars, the end of the Drum Battery, the vulgarisation of O'Connell Bridge with the Tostal's 'Bowl of Light', a dawning awareness of censorship, a crozier's wallop on the heads of all who dared to attend a Yugoslav football match – never mind those who falteringly welcomed the beginnings of a 'pagan' Welfare State in the form of Dr Noel Browne's 'Mother and Child Scheme' – and the perennial 'to Hell or to England' choice of the emigration boats. That decade of the 'grey, tired face' went out with a whimpering obeisance to all-pervading authority and Lemass's new doctrines of modernity and efficiency. We hadn't learned our children's trick of protest, petition, argument and sit-ins when the powers-that-be closed down the Harcourt Street rail-line, did away with the jarvies, built Ballymun, ripped out Victorian pub interiors and replaced them with veneer and plastic, bulldozed our heritage for motorways and – among the worst sacrileges! – did away with the 'the ould Howth tram'.

The Howth tram was not only an institution in its own right, but a way of life. From the date of its gala inauguration in June 1901 until its abysmal closure in May 1959, 'the tram' always retained something of the appeal of a carnival merry-go-round. One half-expected an ornate hurdy-gurdy or steam-organ accompaniment to its jolly, climbing, meandering route through the promontory's spectacular scenery. Dubliners, knowing that on a good summer's day their native bay rivalled the more famous Naples in beauty, saw their Howth tram as the equivalent of the Neapolitan funicular, and recognised that their raucous 'too-ra-lamma, too-ra-lamma' refrains were every bit as good as any imported '*funiculi, funicula*' songs. Edwardian day-trippers, excursionists and picnickers instantly flocked to the new tramway system; working-class honeymooners – with only a bank-holiday weekend at their disposal before returning to their inner-city tenement or 'two-pair-back' – quickly followed suit. For many of them, over the next half century, the Howth tram excursion and picnic was the wedding anniversary or birthday treat.

And what a treat! First in its handsome livery of crimson lake and ivory (highlighted in blue and gold), later in richly varnished mahogony with gold leaf trim and gleaming brass, and finally in the bright blue and cream that my generation remembers, the Howth tram boasted not only the distinction of being the world's tallest 'open-topper' – the high wire cages were to protect the passengers from the many tree branches – but also remained the last of the breed in these islands.

The tram route bisected farms, tunnelled through shelves of golden gorse, burst out on breathtaking views of Dublin Bay, the Wicklow Mountains, Lambay Island and Ireland's Eye, and occasionally (during the clear weather of early morning or the calmness of sunset) met with the distant peaks of the Mourne Mountains and even the tip of Snowden in Wales. And the same tram had all the zinging, clinging, hugging and near-hysterical excitement of a roller coaster. Its route was an adventure trail. Commencing at Sutton Cross Rail Station it tacked over the main road at Sutton Cross with an imperious 'clear the way', clanging its gleaming gong, scattering cyclists, motors, bread vans and Guinness drays, then lurching into the shelter of trees behind the Marine Hotel – taking a breather, as it were – before bracing itself for the full blast of the coastal stretch of the Strand Road. On this exposed stretch (delightful in spring and summer, when the tram sailed proudly by the water, a different story entirely when wintry rain and sea gales lashed over the tiny kerb-high stone wall fronting the beach) the driver had frequently to leap from his seat and dash halfway up the stairs to keep his feet dry. Thereafter, winter or summer, sunshine or snow, the plucky tram wobbled up to the summit, nodding to farmhouses, smiling at passers-by, tooting at tourists, gently clanging, until suddenly – and with a kind of triumphant and insouciant wave of its trolley pole – free-wheeled all the way down to Howth village and the railway station, offering splendid panoramas to its lucky passengers on the way and, in the process, enriching the everyday life of the people.

'The motormen and drivers were generally local men and were virtually controllers and custodians of their own cars', writes Jim Kilroy (who, with his colleagues of the Howth Transport Museum, lovingly and painstakingly rescued and restored the last of the old carriages). 'They knew the regular travellers and would stop anywhere on the line if signalled. They clanged their gongs past certain houses on request, to signal their arrival, and often knocked on doors to hurry along someone likely to be late for work. They looked after children in inclement weather and their courtesy to young and old was legend. Parcels were delivered from one end to the other. Poorer folk were rarely charged the fare and the service was friendly and polite. The Howth peninsula not only lost her trams but also a way of life and a part of her heritage. The ghost of the blue and cream cars can still be seen in the eyes of many gliding silently through the hills. They refuse to be forgotten.'

Jim and his fellow enthusiasts certainly haven't forgotten or neglected that heritage. While the few remaining cars of the Howth tramway are scattered about the world among transport history lovers who valued what we threw aside – the cars are in museums from California to Manchester, Belfast to Derbyshire – it is to the eternal credit of the Howth Transport Museum people that they now have their carriage, resplendant in all its old finery, up and ready for running. This success entailed years of unremitting and voluntary work, and trips to Holland and Denmark to root about old scrapyards for discarded but vital bits and pieces for repair and re-adaptation, and now only requires the laying of a section of track and overhead cable poles in an area of Howth Castle demesne for all the old magic to return. Bord Fáilte and Dublin Tourism, please take note!

From trams, trains and steam engines, this discourse leads to boats. Someone once wrote that 'a successful type of yacht shares with a well-designed steam locomotive the characteristics of longevity. Both those examples of man's handiwork may have their active lives prolonged almost indefinitely, given sufficiently affectionate, skilled and enthusiastic owners' (quoted by Anthony Kavanagh in his excellent 'Sport and Recreation' chapter, *The Howth Peninsula*, Ed. Vincent J. McBrierty, North Dublin Round Table, 1981). As befits an ancient seafaring community, Howth has given its name to a distinctive seventeen-foot sailing boat which is said to be the world's oldest surviving one-design keel boat. Credit for the design goes to Sir Walter Boyd, a founder member of Howth

Sailing Club in 1895, who was asked to design a boat for club use which would cost no more than ninety pounds, was to be raced with a crew of three and yet still be capable of single-handed sailing, containing mainsail, topsail, storm jibs and spinnaker. Boyd successfully carried out the task and had the first five boats, built by J. Hilditch of Carrickfergus, ready for racing in the annual Regatta of 1898. The fleet of seventeen-footers grew to eight over the next decade. Somewhat erroneously termed the 'Dublin Bay 17-footer' after the club of that name adopted the Boyd design in 1906, the keen rivalry between both clubs over the next few years may have had something to do with claim to the title, but it certainly added to the growing reputation of the seventeen-footers (which, oddly enough, never numbered more than a combined fleet of seventeen, as a 1940s project to build the eighteenth boat never came to fruition). In 1967, some seventy years after Howth's first commodore sketched his now legendary design, the 17 Foot Association was formed, and now all remaining boats in that class are based at Howth and compete regularly in the picturesque rig with which they were first launched almost a century ago.

Howth, like Lough Shinney, Rush and Portmarnock, was always a good place to avoid too many encounters with the 'grey, tired face' of the 1950s. In memory it was always sunny. Once, with Joe Dillon and Mick Wright, now a successful fish merchant on the West Pier, I hired a rowing boat and we made it over to Ireland's Eye. I think our intention was to locate the 'Long Hole' where (exactly a century before) the artist William Kirwan was alleged to have murdered his wife. An air of mystery still surrounds the strange death of the pretty twenty-eight-year-old Maria, and the subsequent trial of her husband was a *cause célèbre* of Victorian Dublin. Maria's dead body was found lying on a jagged rock in the tidal waters of the Long Hole. Apparently, she had gone swimming while her husband was engrossed in his painting. The boatmen who rowed over in the evening to fetch the Kirwans found the distraught artist wandering about in search of his wife. After nearly two hours, and in the dusk, the boatmen stumbled on the body in the Long Hole (which, at high tide, has about five feet of water and less than an ankle-high trickle at low tide). The inquest the next day returned a verdict of 'found drowned'.

The matter might have ended there had not rumours telling of a woman's voice screaming in distress (and drifting over the channel to the mainland that fateful evening) coincided with the fact that a few weeks after his wife's death Kirwan brought his mistress into his Upper Merrion Street home. Howth wasn't *that* isolated or remote from the city! The corpse was exhumed and a post mortem examination overturned the inquest verdict with the revelation that death wasn't due to drowning but by the body having been pierced by a sharp object. A jagged piece of stone at the Long Hole? Or an artist's palette knife or pencil-sharpening penknife? Kirwan was subsequently arrested, charged with murder and found guilty. He protested his innocence to the end: 'I solemnly declare in the presence of this court and of that God before whom I must soon appear, that I had neither act or part in the death of the late Mrs Kirwan and I will further declare that I never treated her unkindly.'

Due largely to the efforts of his defence counsel, the formidable Isaac Butt (who had drawn attention to quite a few discrepancies in the case for the prosecution), Kirwan's death sentence was commuted at the eleventh hour to imprisonment for thirty years. On his release in 1879, an old and broken man, he returned briefly and quietly to the scene of his wife's death before departing for America. Some say that he went there to join his mistress of yore; others say that he took with him the dark secret of the 'murder on Ireland's Eye' – or the mystery death at the 'Body Rock'?

On that bright September evening of 1952 my amateur sleuthing companions and I searched in vain for the macabre Long Hole. We raced over a loose shingle of small pebbles that gradually became an uneven medley of slippery boulders. The boulders grew alarmingly in size, so that what began as a series of hops and jumps ended in a tedious and tiring scaling over massive rocks. The tide was swirling in below us. The hired boat that we had so carelessly beached on a little strip of dry sand now had its stern slowly rising and falling in a near foot of water. One of the casually tossed aside oars was being steadily sucked off the sand and was making ready for a haphazard voyage to the Isle of Man, or God knows where. Dillon yelled a warning. We quickly scrambled and splashed and knee-scraped a hurried route back to our half-floating craft before it coursed away to the Azores. We made it just in time. Afterwards, in the comfort of the Abbey Tavern – or was it the Cock Tavern on Church Hill? – we were reminded of how lucky we'd just been when an old-timer regaled us with tales of drownings and shipwreck disasters that all but banished the Kirwan story from our minds.

Since those days I've occasionally thought what a dreadful, even traumatic, decade the 1850s must have been for some of those older seaward-peering people of Howth's remote little fishing village. The noisy, smokey and cinder-belching rail engines were still in their infancy – scarcely five years had elapsed since they'd begun snorting their way across the narrow and sandy isthmus of Sutton – and now they were regularly unloading such unlikely people as the raffish artist Kirwan and his hapless wife. Almost immediately in their wake came another type of artist: the sensation-seeking hack from the pre-photography London papers, anxious to sketch the scene of the crime. Ireland's Eye, the Long Hole and the Body Rock were quickly and Gothicly illustrated. In even greater numbers the same *London Illustrated* reporters and artists were back again in February for the next sensation, the wreck of the packet *Queen Victoria* on Casana Rock with the loss of sixty lives. The hero of the day was the vigilant and quick-thinking Captain Brown of the *Roscommon*, on route from Dublin to Holyhead, who raced through the snowstorm to the scene, lowered his boats and rescued over fifty people.

The real scoop came in January of the following year, 1854, with the loss of the *Tayleur* off Lambay Island, a maritime disaster that curiously and tragically prefigured the *Titanic* disaster sixty years later. 'The largest sailing merchantman ever built' (with a cargo-carrying capacity of 4,000 tons and a passenger and crew complement of 700), the *Tayleur* was constructed expressly for the Australian emigrant and gold-rush trade. On its maiden voyage (and again, like the *Titanic*, with a combination of over-confidence, poor communication between officers and crew and, above all, adverse weather conditions) the great ship was needlessly smashed to smithereens on the easterly reef of Lambay. The vast majority of its 589 passengers, crew and 'five stowaways' were either drowned or violently dashed to death on the sharp rocks, with only 'three women out of 200 on board being saved'.

It is difficult for us nowadays to imagine that news of the shocking disaster didn't reach Dublin until nearly twenty-four hours later due to the 'remoteness of Lambay Island and the awful weather'! The *Tayleur* struck the reef at about noon on Saturday, 21 January and it was not until Sunday afternoon that a rescue ship (the City of Dublin steam packet *Prince*) sped to the island to search for survivors. Also speeding to the scene were the inevitable news-hounds and graphic artists. The *Illustrated London News* a week later gave some harrowing eye-witness accounts:

> . . . the ship began to sink by the stern and the sense of confusion and dismay that ensued baffles all description; the passengers rushing up the hatchway – husbands carrying their children, and women lying prostrate on the deck with their infants, screaming and imploring help . . . those who attempted to escape by the bows of the vessel all, or nearly, met a miserable fate. The moment they fell into the water the waves caught them and dashed them violently against the rocks and the survivors on shore could perceive the unfortunate creatures, with their heads bruised and cut open, struggling amidst the waves and one by one sinking under them.

The pubs in Howth were once full of such dark tales from salty old-timers. The massive wreck of the *Tayleur* lay undisturbed and undiscovered for over a century, a silent and watery sea-grave on the sandy bottom between Lambay's Nose and the 'Sea Hole', a tract of water known ever since as Tayleur Bay. In July 1959 divers of the nascent Irish Sub-Acqua Club located it after more than a season of fruitless and haphazard searching. It might seem that with a keel of 210 feet, a forty-foot beam and with lofty masts for a huge spread of canvas, the *Tayleur*'s skeleton should have been discernible on the seabed. This was not the case. Poor visibility after the first few feet of a diver's submersion plus a hundred years of gentle, yet relentless silting and seaweeding of the shattered merchantman blurred, if not completely obliterated, the ghostly outlines of the death ship. How then was it finally located?

It was my old friend and neighbour of Artane days, Ronnie Warren (one of the sub-acqua diving team) who told me that they were almost on the point of giving up their search when a chance encounter with an old-timer in a pub helped to pin-point the actual location. The old salt mentioned that he regularly laid down lobster pots all around Lambay. In one specific area the pots he hauled up contained rust-tinted sand, a sure sign of a major wreck below. The very next Sunday he conducted the weekend underwater and amateur sleuths to the spot. Within an hour the divers had located the wreck. Forget your scientific measurements, Admiralty charts, tidal data, old newspaper research – an old fisherman's yarn and a solitary lobster-pot of reddish sand had provided the important clue! Within a season later the weekend divers had retrieved the ship's binnacle (the box containing the ship's compass), important parts of the steering mechanism, a large amount of Victorian pottery and porcelain vessels and the *Tayleur's* encrusted bell – the same that had clanged so forlornly and so futilely on that dreadful January day so long ago.

One hundred and fifty years ago D'Alton, the great historian of our country, said of Howth: 'Were it within six times the distance from London that it is from Dublin, it would long before this be a diadem of picturesque attraction.' Ninety years ago another historian, Dillon Cosgrave, wrote: 'There is no place near Dublin more assured of a prosperous future than Howth. Nor is this wonderful. It is the gem of Fingal; and may even be described as the most beautiful place near Dublin. Here is the great attraction to a citizen of escape from roads, and the still greater of hills, vales and streams, furze, fern, and heather.'

Many would say that Howth has indeed prospered; some might dispute the assertion. Yet all would agree, I'm sure, that it still remains one of the gems of Fingal and one of the most beautiful places near Dublin. And for me, in Howth, there always lies, along with the golden memories associated with the visible world of such beauty, an invisible world of old, fearful and heroic tales . . . and the ghostly rumble of an old tram all tricked out in ice-cream colours.

· 8 ·

Donnybrook

DURING the years of 1939–45 when I was growing up, there really wasn't much opportunity to travel, unless, of course, it was to England either to enlist or to find work in the munition factories. And it really didn't have all that much to do with the war, or the Emergency, as we called it here in Ireland. No, economics as much as global conflict kept people close to home.

But my brothers and I – and most of our gang – had bicycles of sorts. We were northsiders, and if the limits of our horizon were the Phoenix Park to the west, the Bull Island to the east, the country villages of Swords and Malahide to the north, and the Liffey to the south, we nonetheless had a wonderful and varied world to explore. My older brother Jack was our leader, map-reader, explorer-in-chief. It was he who lead us on our first glorious invasion of the foreign lands south of the Liffey. The occasion was the great Military Tattoo and Exhibition mounted by the Defence Forces and held at the RDS Grounds, Ballsbridge, at the end of the Emergency. Thus we discovered the Dodder. Further explorations were planned.

One Sunday morning we set out to find a place called Donnybrook. Like so many great expeditions in history, ours was frought with mishaps and danger: little Noel kept slipping off Jack's crossbar; we got lost a number of times (this, mind you, in no way reflected on our navigator's competence but was solely attributable to the haphazard manner in which these peculiar southsiders arranged their streets and roadways); also, two of the expedition's bikes had chains which kept falling off, and we got a puncture, or, to use the parlance of our adventures, 'one of the mustangs had thrown a shoe'. We were halted on a broad 'posh' road attending to the crippled mustang when an elderly gent with a walking stick came over and very kindly showed us how to get the tube back into the tyre without nicking it. He asked us where we came from. We told him, adding that we were 'kind of explorin', like'.

'Explorers, eh?' He gave a little half-smile, and then, with the tip of his walking cane, pointed up the road. 'Know who used to live up there? Sixth or seventh house, I think. No? Well, number 35 used to be the home of Sir Ernest Shackleton, the great Antarctic explorer. Ever heard of him?'

No, we hadn't. Very briefly, but graphically, the gent with the walking stick told us of Shackleton's voyage in the *Endurance* in 1914 and of his attempt to cross the mountains of the Antarctic. It was a tale of heroism that held us enthralled – a saga of a great ship, the *Endurance*, crushed by the ice of the Weddel Sea, of Shackleton's party escaping in boats to Elephant Island, and then, in an open boat and with only a few companions, Shackleton braving a thousand miles of icy ocean to seek help for those companions he'd been compelled to leave behind on Elephant Island. When he struck land at South Georgia Island there followed a nightmarish hike across the snow-capped summit to alert rescuers at a Norwegian whaling station. It was the very stuff of valour and adventure; we vividly saw Shackleton and his companions, starving, bedraggled and half-frozen, stumbling in on the incredulous whalers and blurting out their tale of an epic voyage and appealing for help for their comrades.

When the gent with the walking stick had departed we pushed our bikes up the road and stood with a kind of awed hero-worship before a rather ordinary-looking Victorian terrace house with high steps leading up to the front door. In later years we read more of the Antarctic exploration and of Ernest Shackleton's exploits. He was a veteran of Scott's 1902 Discovery expedition (which pushed within 575 miles of the South Pole), when he led a party to Antarctica in 1908 hoping to reach both the South Pole and the south magnetic pole. Fighting blizzards and illness, Shackleton and the main party trekked 1,730 miles and got as close as ninety-seven miles to the South Pole. Their position, eighty-eight degrees south latitude, became the new 'farthest south'. In 1910 Scott's second expedition set out but was beaten in the race to the pole by the

Norwegian, Roald Amundsen. The race for the South Pole was over, but that didn't stop Shackleton from setting out again in 1914 in the *Endurance*, this time to cross the mountains of the Antarctic continent. This was the year of Shackleton's abandoning the *Endurance* in the ice of the Weddel Sea and of his heroic dash to South Georgia Island. His fourth expedition, in the *Quest*, was abandoned when he died suddenly at Grytviken, South Georgia, in 1922, aged forty-eight. His wife had Shackleton's body buried on the island under the shadow of the formidable range of mountains which he had been first to cross. One feels, with his wife, that this is what Shackleton would have wished. He loved Antarctica.

It was only when I read quite recently John Cowell's *Where They Lived in Dublin* (O'Brien Press, 1980) that I learned two supplementary pieces of information. One was that Shackleton was born at Kilkea House, County Kildare, on 15 February 1874, the very same day that the first-ever photographs of the massive icebergs of Antarctica were taken from the deck of the *Challenger*. The voyage of this steamship – the largest ship until then ever to enter Antarctic waters – also established beyond doubt that a vast continent, upon which humans had never set foot, lay further to the south. The date of 15 February – coincidence, or fate?

I also learned from John Cowell's book the name of that road in Donnybrook where Ernest Shackleton had lived for six years as a schoolboy: Marlborough Road. That name – though not the memory of an elderly gent with a walking stick and a stirring tale! – had eluded me for years. So you see, we intrepid explorers from the northside – on our trusty 'mustangs' and with our tattered map of strange territories to the south of the Liffey – made some very worthwhile voyages and discoveries in our time too, didn't we?

I've always been greatly interested, indeed fascinated, by the subtle 'art of putting things'. Let me give you an instance: my eighty-year-old bedraggled copy of *Harmsworth*

Encyclopaedia, in describing the 1855 demise of the ancient and time-honoured festivals of Donnybrook Fair (Dublin) and Bartholomew Fair (London), states that the former was suppressed because of its 'riotous behaviour', whereas the latter was merely abolished as 'a nuisance'.

Get it? The Jackeens were 'drunk, disorderly and outrageous', the Cockneys merely 'high spirited'. It would be difficult, of course, to deny the charge of riotous behaviour, yet Constantia Maxwell in *Dublin Under The Georges* says:

> Barrington and other Irish writers prided themselves on the fact that there were fewer thieves, swindlers, or pickpockets at this typically Irish festival than at St Bartholomew's Fair in London. This is probably true, for at Donnybrook little actual money changed hands.

And the German Prince Puckler-Muskau, who paid a visit to Donnybrook Fair during his Dublin sojourn of 1828, wrote to a friend as follows:

> Nothing indeed can be more national. The poverty, the dirt, and the wild tumult were as great as the glee and merriment with which the cheapest pleasures were enjoyed . . . not the slightest trace of English brutality was to be perceived: they were more like French people, though their gaiety was mingled with more humour and more genuine good nature; both of which are national traits of the Irish, and are always doubled by potheen.

The original fair was established by Royal Charter in 1204 when King John compensated the Dublin citizens for the expense of building defensive walls around the city and permitted them to hold an annual eight-day fair in the little village of Donnybrook. For centuries it ranked highly among the great European fairs as an important trading centre. Merchants travelled to it from many foreign countries to transact their business. Along with the various commodities, livestock and farm produce were sold at the fair, while artisans, physicians, apothecaries, goldsmiths and money-lenders set up their various stalls and booths. The European wars of the sixteenth and seventeenth centuries – not to mention our own homegrown variety! – gradually diminished the international and commercial importance of Donnybrook Fair. By the eighteenth century it had degenerated into a bacchanalian fun fair. Dancing, carousing, music, rough-and-ready equestrian sport and faction fights were the order of the day. And love-making prevailed: one local priest averred that more marriages were celebrated in Dublin the week after the fair than in any two months during the rest of the year!

By the early 1800s the colourful carnival booths had given way to crude wattle-and-sod affairs covered with old quilts, winnowing sheets, sacks and canvas. Inside, benches or planks were stretched along the sides for seating, and old doors and wooden beams (raised on mounds of earth and sod) formed a continuous table down the centre. At such makeshift tables the company sat, eating, drinking and singing lustily to the strain of fiddle and bagpipes. On turf fires built up near the tent door 'neat victuals' were cooked – Dublin Bay herrings, corned beef, bacon, potatoes, cabbage – while some of the pots contained 'promiscuous edibles' broken up into small portions, pigs' and sheeps' feet, potatoes, turnips, beef and mutton bones. From these 'bubbling hell-broths' the public were invited to try their luck at fishing out some delectability with a long-handled fork, at the rate of 'three prods in the pot for a penny'. And for the gentry, who came a-wenching or to see the sideshow curiosities or the bareknuckle prizefighters, a cold round or rump of beef was provided at 'double price'.

The great bareknuckle champions were Dan Donnelly, Jack Langan and Dan Dougherty; they set up their boxing booths and stripped to the waist and challenged all and sundry to go a few rounds of sparring with the 'raw 'uns', meaning bare fists. Shillelagh and blackthorn stick battles were also part of the attraction. 'No one was disfigured thereby or rendered fit for a doctor', Barrington tells us; 'small hurts were frequent, but did not interfere with the song, the dance, the frolicking or general good humour'.

Weston St John Joyce puts it somewhat differently:

> Every year on the approach of Fair time (26th August), large sums of money were withdrawn from the savings banks in Dublin to be squandered in drunkenness, gambling and other dissipations; all business was in a state of partial suspension for weeks together: every anniversary was signalised by numerous cases of personal injuries if not by actual loss of life, and in some instances even epidemics were ascribed to the Fair.
>
> Servants, mechanics, shop assistants, tradesmen and clerks visiting the place, were drawn into the vortex of dissipation, and losing their money, their situations and their characters, swelled the numbers of the unemployed in the city, and drifted thence into crime.

As the city spread outwards in the middle years of the last century the new suburbanites took vigorous action to rid themselves of this annual nuisance on their doorstep. A press campaign was launched, a subscription list opened, and finally in 1855 the patent for the fair was purchased from its owners for £3,000 and was allowed to lapse. For a few years afterwards a local publican persisted in holding a miniature fair of sorts on his property, but in 1859 the magistrates put a stop to his gallop by refusing to renew his licence.

Still, it's hard to kill a bad thing. For some years after the suppression of the fair, a number of city folk annually assembled on the Fair Green on its anniversary (26 August) and then did a round of the village taverns. With time even this half-hearted practice fell into disuse. A hundred years later – almost on the centenary of the fair's abolition – there was one brief, final, muted echo of the old spirit of Donnybrook riotousness. The occasion was the Billy Kelly-Ray Famechon European Featherweight Title fight of May 1955; the venue was Donnybrook Bus Depot, built on part of the old Fair Green. Seven thousand Irishmen packed the vast temporary arena to cheer their champion to victory. When Kelly lost on a disputed decision, a number of the spectators vented their feelings by tossing a few of the fold-up chairs into the ring. It was a tame, half-jocous protest – not at all like the 'wild tumults' of the past. Donnybrook Fair as a riotous assembly was most assuredly dead and buried . . . and gone forever.

The modern 360-foot RTE transmitter mast at Donnybrook casts a long and slender shadow. It slants across the stonework and the roof of an old mansion in the grounds below it. When the mansion was built 160 years ago radio and television were undreamt of. Yet, the long shadow touching the old house links the past and the present in one of those curious and happy coincidences of history that never fail to delight me.

The mansion – Montrose – was built in 1836 by the Dublin distiller James Jameson. Of Scottish descent, Jameson had a great liking for the novels of Sir Walter Scott, hence the name Montrose for his new home. His daughter Anne had an even stronger liking for the Italian operas based on Scott's romantic tales, hence her determination to go to Italy to study music. At Bologna Anne Jameson met and fell in love with a wealthy estate owner named Giuseppe Marconi. They married in 1864. Their second son, Guglielmo, was born ten years later. He grew up to be a delicate and studious child, reading widely in the excellent scientific library at Villa Grifone, the Marconi home. He became very interested in the study of electromagnetic waves. To him the possibility of wireless telegraphy was so real that he could not understand his father's 'poo-pooing' the whole idea.

Anne was different. She permitted Guglielmo and his brother Alfonso to set up their homemade apparatus in the attic. It was here one day, when Guglielmo successfully managed to transmit a faint message to Alfonso at the far end of the room, that wireless telegraphy was born. And it was Anne who next encouraged her son to fix up his equipment on the grounds of the estate so that he might experiment further by sending and receiving signals by electrical waves over a longer distance than had ever been done before.

The Italian government showed very little interest in the twenty-year-old Marconi's discoveries; so, in 1896, Anne accompanied Guglielmo to London to help him seek capital for a wireless telegraph company and to assist him in applying for and receiving the first wireless patent, the famous number

7777, from the British government. Marconi's patent was partly based on the theory that the distance of communication increases rapidly as the aerial height is increased. On the roof of London's GPO he first demonstrated his apparatus to the Post Office chiefs, and in the following year he formed the first wireless company. Marconi's company began by installing wireless sets in lightships off the English coast. In April 1899 – scarcely a month after Marconi had sent his first wireless telegraph message across the English Channel, a distance of eighty-five miles – the East Goodwin lightship was pounded by heavy seas and part of its deckhouse was swept away. The stricken vessel sent an urgent SOS to a nearby station and help arrived just in time. Thus radio was used for the very first time to save life at sea.

In 1901 Marconi, at his first attempt, succeeded in transmitting and receiving signals across the Atlantic, and in the next year demonstrated that wireless signals can be received over greater distances at night than in daytime. Thereafter further successes and honours followed: in 1909 Marconi shared the Nobel prize in Physics with Braun for their development of radio, was nominated by the King of Italy to the Italian Senate for life, sent the first message from Britain to Australia in 1918, and picked up a second Nobel prize the following year, as well as the Albert Medal of the Royal Society of Arts and many other prestigious foreign decorations and scientific awards. He was created a *marchese* by King Victor Immanuel in 1929.

Right up until his death in 1937 Marconi never ceased to honour the memory of his mother and to give credit to Anne Jameson of Montrose for all her steadfast encouragement. He was proud of his Irish connections too and once wrote the following words to H. S. Doig, editor of the *Dublin Express* and *Evening Mail*:

> I remember very well the enterprise shown by the *Dublin Express* in availing itself, for the first time, of my system of wireless telegraphy to report the Kingstown Regattas in 1898 and, as soon as arrangements shall have been made for the exchange of press wireless telephonic messages between Ireland and the United States or Canada, I will bear in mind the wish you express that the *Dublin Express*

shall be one of the first to avail itself of this new method of communication,

Yours faithfully,
G. Marconi.

This meeting of extremes at Montrose – a sturdy nineteenth-century mansion and a lofty, ultra-modern piece of high-technology – has a touching appropriateness. They are like markers to an inspiring human story; the mast that gives evidence of a son's ability to 'put a girdle round about the earth' stands protectively over a mother's birthplace. The old house has the exclusive air of an elderly Victorian lady. But she is an old lady who has been pressed into service as an office worker for Ireland's television and radio network. She seems in no way displeased with her lot. In fact, the old lady seems immensely proud.

Donnybrook – *Domhnach Broc*, site of an ancient monastic settlement on the banks of the Dodder – was for generations the land held by the Gaelic clan of Mac Gillamocholmog. Then the Normans came, a small band of armoured men on horseback, aristocratic in their pretensions, ruthless adventurers, skilled in the arts of warfare, and lead by the fearless Walter De Ridelford, the Lord of Bray and the staunchest of Strongbow's lieutenants. With his mounted warriors in chain mail, his men-at-arms and his Welsh bowmen, Sir Walter routed the Gaelic clansmen.

And to the victors, the spoils! The Norman method was to conquer, build stout and graceless defensive towers, have vassels and villeins work the captured land, and then make an endowment to Mother Church in thanksgiving to the Almighty for having blessed the bloody work of sword and longbow. It was a policy of aggrandisement exalted to the realm of a holy crusade. But how to hold onto such lands? When De Ridelford died, the lands of Donnybrook, along with all his other possessions, were inherited by his little granddaughter, Christina De Marisco. Thus the stage was set for dark intrigues and a tale of woe. To prevent this property from passing out of the domain of the Crown,

Henry II bestowed the hand of the rich heiress on one of his henchmen, Fulk of Newcastle, Christina's appointed guardian.

We know the scene: a score of Norman men-at-arms and emissaries ride towards the Dodder through the rain and mud. They are bearing gifts and a handsome proposal that scarcely shrouds a threat. They are riding to the betrothal ceremony of Fulk and Christina. But the bride-to-be is no 'lone virgin of marriageable age'; she is a mere child of two years, immensely rich, however, and therefore a hapless pawn in the complex dynastic scheme. The horsemen ford the Dodder, clattering up to the stone keep and calling loudly. A massive door swings open – inside the walls there is a huge fire of logs and peat, the flames casting fantastic shadows into the corners of the great hall, brightening the rough-hewn stones and making more ruddy the red of wine shining in the raised glasses and tankards. On a great oaken table there are unfurled parchments and, under the tilt of a guttering candle, red wax melting for the affixing of seals and the making of a heartless contract. Gruff speeches follow and hearty, back-slapping congratulations, and there is much toasting and quaffing of wine as a waif's future is sealed and her adult years blithely disposed of with a quick flourish of a goose quill.

The rain continues outside, wailing against the stones. Upstairs – somewhere in the shadowy reaches of a grim tower – Christina De Marisco is alone in her cot. It is dark. The child is weeping.

Seven years pass. What a lot can happen in the turbulent days of marching men and border frays! Fulk of Newcastle is no longer a claimant for Christina's hand. Dead, murdered, or shouldered out of the way by more ruthless and ambitious men, we don't know. We do know, however, that the nine-year-old Christina is now compelled to marry another suitor, Ebulo De Geneve. The medieval chronicler, Robert of Gloucester, captures something of the mood of such heiresses in his lines:

> 'Sir,' quoth she, 'well I note that your heart upon me is more for mine heritage, than for myself . . .'

Added to Christina's plight is a child's ignorance of the

world of men and of the wider world beyond her prison. We shall never really understand her heart, but there are sad glimpses of her at a castle window, her hair about her shoulders, her voice sobbing and begging for help from her nurse and her few loyal friends. Then, as if the drama had not been exhausted, we suddenly learn of her flight, riding through the night disguised as a page boy, escaping in an open boat to France, there to throw herself on the mercy of Eleanor of Acquitaine, widow of Henry II. In far-off Normandy there is peace, but at a price. Christina is permitted to enter a convent on condition that she relinquish her entire estate to the Crown. It is a price the child is prepared to pay; with a touching eagerness she accepts. The veil offers anonymity, the cloister becomes a sanctuary from the brutal machinations of greedy men.

Christina De Marisco's inheritance duly passed to the Crown, and thence to the King's Deputy, Lord Edward Baggot, in 1254. And still the dispossessed clansmen waited, watchful, and looked down from their mountains to the south, so Lord Edward built a much stronger castle at a place which became known as Baggot Rath. There was need for such castles 'where fear drove comfort out' for nigh on 500 years as the lords of Donnybrook came and went, first the Baggots, then the Fitzwilliams and then their kinsmen through marriage, the Usshers.

When John Ussher became Lord Mayor of Dublin in the sixteenth century he built Donnybrook Castle. It was said of such Norman and Anglo-Irish magnates that 'they dreamed not of a perishable home, who thus could build' – and yet practically all of their bleak and defensive fortresses were to suffer the ravages of war and time, were to crumble into ruins, or be dismantled for other, less warlike, houses. Donnybrook Castle, modified to the more refined tastes of the eighteenth century, became the home of the Stoyte family, who frequently entertained their friends Dean Swift and Esther Johnson (Stella) there.

I like to give my imagination reign and to picture the paternalistic Dean walking arm-in-arm with Stella by the banks of the Dodder, her hair 'blacker than a raven, and every feature of her face in perfection' as she listens attentively to his discourses. Might he have told Stella, 'one of the most beautiful, graceful, and agreeable young women', the sad tale of Christina De Marisco? By the 1790s (long after Stella and Swift were dead) the castle was in a ruinous state and a smaller house was built on its site. This latter house with its adjoining lands was purchased in 1837 by Mother Mary Aikenhead, foundress of the Irish Sisters of Charity, and it became the St Mary Magdelen Home of Refuge.

I never pass by the convent gates at Donnybrook without thinking of another home of refuge – in another age, another place – and of a fishing smack bound for France, tossed about in the wild sea and taking a frightened child away from nine years of sorrow. The latter years of Christina De Marisco's life are obscure. I hope she found the peace and serenity denied to her as a consequence of her inheritance. I like to think she did. Her tears had seeped into the stones of a grim Norman tower at Donnybrook for too long. A cloistered, sunlit garden in Normandy deserved to echo with her laughter.

· 9 ·

Sandymount

SANDYMOUNT is a great place to approach. Its quiet avenues and pretty gardens beckon you on. Your heart goes out to it. Something of the serenity and good manners of the age of the horse-and-carriage, or the electric trams, leads you into its core. The mark of the tram tracks is still discernible on Gilford Road. Under the layer of tarmacadam they can clearly be seen curving into the gateway of the Brunswick Press, a printing premises which was formerly the site of the tram sheds, some of which are still there.

Sandymount seems always to have attracted or produced eminent Irish writers. As a maritime suburb it appears to be constantly grasping a pen and leaning over a writing desk, or twirling an ink-stained quill in contemplation as it gazes out to sea. Something in the air must operate wonderfully to aid the Muse, never failing to be romantic and inspiring. The most celebrated of Ireland's poets, W. B. Yeats (1865–1939), was born at Sandymount Avenue, and the 1923 Nobel prize winner for literature has his connection with the area commemorated by a bust in Sandymount Green. Frank O'Conner (1903–66), novelist and short-story writer, had lodgings at Sandymount Green when he first came to live in Dublin in the late 1920s. He later lived for a time at 57 Strand Road, which was once the home of the famous Shakespearean actor Anew McMaster and is now the home of artist Desmond McCarthy. T. C. Murray (1873–1959), one of the greatest of the Abbey Theatre playwrights and a sharp critic of the quiet desperation and tragedy of Irish rural life in his time, lived at 11 Sandymount Avenue.

Even those former denizens of Sandymount who are much better remembered as patriots and politicians – Charles Kickham, James Stephens, Padraig Pearse and Eamon De Valera – have all proven their abilities as writers. Kickham and Stephens were Tipperary men and Fenian conspirators who lived incognito at Fairfield House, Sandymount, for a few months in 1865 while Dublin Castle spies tried to ferret out their whereabouts. Stephens's alias of 'Mr Herbert' was in all probability suggested by the fact that Fairfield House stood at the junction of Herbert Road and Newbridge Avenue. Whether or not Kickham affected the alias of 'Mr Newbridge' is uncertain, but both were detected and subsequently arrested. Kickham was the author of the still-popular novel *Knocknagow* and Stephens the translator of Dickens's *Martin Chuzzlewit* into the French language while he was a political emigré in Paris after his escape from Richmond Prison.

And it was to his aunt's home on Strand Road that the young James Joyce fled after Gogarty's fusillade of revolver shots had evicted him from the Sandycove Martello tower in September 1904. Joyce wrote at the time: 'I had nothing to rely on but myself.' Hardly fair to the aunt and her hospitality, was it? Still in the same mood the next day, Joyce wrote to Nora Barnacle and asked her to 'stand beside' him and to go abroad with him. Nora agreed. The rest is literary history.

In Zurich, ten years later, Joyce was well into the early chapters of *Ulysses*. Dublin still dominated his thoughts. He wrote to his aunt and to members of his family for minute details: were there trees, and if so of what kind, behind the Star of the Sea Church in Sandymount? The family obliged with all the necessary information. Thereafter Sandymount figured prominently in his masterpiece:

> . . . the gentleman off Sandymount green that Cissy Caffrey called the man that was so like himself passing along the strand taking a short walk . . . the lamp-lighter would be going his rounds past the presbyterian church grounds and along by shady Tritonville avenue where the couples walked . . . She loathed that sort of person, the fallen women off the accommodation walk beside the Dodder that went with soldiers and coarse men . . .

Joyce took Sandymount up out of the leisurely suburban world, for which it was so well designed, and dedicated it to the literature of the ages. Its avenues, its trees and its timeless sands enjoy the kind of strange immortality which comes from having been observed and annotated by a genius.

O'Connor and Beckett have likewise managed to work something of their appreciation of Sandymount into their literary output. O'Connor tells how (on his reluctant arrival in Dublin and hoping for an early return to his native Cork) he was appointed to the municipal library at Ballsbridge and stayed in 'digs in Sandymount Green, in a big house kept by a Donegal man and his sister who had retired to enjoy themselves in the great city'. Beckett, though never actually a resident of Sandymount as far as I know, mentions the place in his poem 'Serena III' and also in his unpublished first novel *Dream of Fair to Middling Women*, written in a Paris hotel in 1932 and excerpts of which have appeared from time to time in a number of books on Beckett.

> Slow down slink down the Ringsend Road
> Irishtown Sandymount puzzle find the Hell Fire.

And:

> . . . a little single-decker bound for Sandymount Tower, cried up to him from the causeway of Nassau Street, and passed.

The reference to the single-decker is a reminder that the first double-decker bus did not appear on the Dublin streets until 1937, and that the pair of bridges at South Lotts Road and Bath Avenue (the latter leading by a circuitous route to the bus and tram terminus at Sandymount Martello Tower) were so low that no double-decker tram or bus could pass under them.

And thus I'm lead from a brief note on Sandymount's illustrious authors to a description of its buses and trams, so why shouldn't I conclude with the following item from an anonymous Sandymount scribe who penned these lines to the Letters page of the now defunct *Dublin Evening Mail* of 1940:

> She could not find her tramcar fare,
> The conductor was not rough,
> She kissed him sweetly then and
> there
> And he said, 'Fair enough!'

Didn't I tell you that Sandymount seems always to have attracted and produced great writers? Why, even the humble tram passenger had the makings of a poet!

And I must confess to a peculiar satisfaction whenever I see the names of the forgotten or lesser-known figures in our city's history recorded in street names or on houses. O'Connell, Parnell and Pearse streets are all very well – everyone knows or has read something of the historical and patriotic personages who are thus recorded by having a major thoroughfare named in their honour; but what of the names appearing on back alley plaques or obscure terraces? The shyest or drabbest building or roadway cannot but feel flattered to be turned into a living remembrance of some little-known character from our city's past.

In Sandymount, for instance, there are quite a few such names to which I am keenly aware. Hepenstall Terrace and Cranfield Place are two. The first recalls the Hepenstall sisters who, in the 1830s (and partly from the proceeds of funds advanced by the Lord Lieutenant), ran a private school for 'respectable young ladies' of the area. The second recalls Richard Cranfield, proprietor of Cranfield's Sea Baths, who died in 1859. Forgive me, but I have a picture of the Misses Hepenstall – refined gentlewomen with complexions as pale as marble, severely attired, well-meaning, dedicated, prudent, practical, but prim and atrociously genteel. And Cranfield? Red-faced and balding, I'd say, with luxuriant side-whiskers and a gold watch chain stretched handsomely across the ample paunch straining against his silken waistcoat.

When Dr Richard Russel 'invented' sea bathing for health and hygiene in the 1750s, and when the Prince Regent took a liking to the bracing sea air of Brighton after his first visit in 1783, bathing resorts became the fashionable rage. It only required the coming of the railways fifty years later to quickly transport the fashionable rage hither and thither and to turn a hundred sleepy fishing villages into pleasure resorts. Sandymount was no exception. And Mr Richard Cranfield recognised a good thing when he saw it.

So did the railway. They built their own baths along the line and conveyed fare-paying passengers to and fro for the privilege of bathing free of charge. However, like the respectable

Victorians that they were, the rail directors made one very important stipulation, and that was 'the building of high walls in front of all the public bathing places along the line, so as to prevent such bathing places and the persons bathing therein from being exposed to the view of passengers on the said railroad'. The high walls were all very well, but there was the devil to pay one afternoon when a group of outraged Victorian matrons stormed into Westland Row Station and reported to the authorities there that they had just seen a whole group of railway construction workers, during their midday lunch break, diving and swimming and generally cavorting on the beach not too far from Sandymount . . . and in the nude!

I have not the slightest doubt, however, that the refined Hepenstall sisters at all times very assiduously shepherded the 'respectable young ladies' who were their pupils away from the gentlemens' bathing places, run by that common trades person, Mr Richard Cranfield.

Where were Scald Hill, Brickfield town, the Conniving House? They are place names that have the rough ring of history about them, and I know of few such which illustrate more vividly something of the past and give us a glimpse of the activities of our ancestors.

Scald Hill was the name given to the narrow tract of land along the sea from Ringsend to Sandymount. In the seventeenth century it was for the most part surrounded by water on both sides. Sir Bernard De Gomme's map of 1673 shows the waters of the Dodder flowing out at low tide in broad streams, 'winding in devious courses through a labyrinth of sands'. Before the Liffey was channelled between its walls it splayed out to meet the Dodder and, at full tide, the sea covered most of the land to the west of Irishtown. Even as late as 1820 Duncan's map shows a lake south of Sandymount Tower, on the low ground adjoining the present Sydney Parade. So then, 300 years ago, at high tide, Scald Hill must have been something of an isthmus connecting the spit of land at Ringsend and Irishtown to Merrion and Booterstown.

The seaward side of Scald Hill was noted for its cockles and shrimp, the latter 'being found in great quantities at certain states of the tide'. Weston St John Joyce in *The Neighbourhood of Dublin* (1913) states:

> . . . but after the severe winter of 1741, known as 'The hard frost', they (the shrimps) completely disappeared and never since returned to this coast. The cockles, however, still remain for those who have the courage to eat them, and occasionally yield a rich harvest to the professional cockle pickers. Going to Sandymount on Sunday to pick cockles was a favourite amusement of the Dublin folk a hundred years ago.

And how did the Dublin folk of the day make their way out to distant Sandymount? Many walked, naturally, but others travelled by way of 'noddy and jingle'. Both were horse-drawn vehicles peculiar to the Dublin streets of that time – low, single, two-wheeled chaises, capable of just about holding two people, with a seat for the driver on the shafts. They were so called from their 'nodding', oscillating movement. One foreign visitor described them as follows:

> . . . they have an odd kind of hacknies here, that is called a Noddy, which is nothing more than an old cast-off one horse chaise or chair, with a kind of stool fixed upon the shafts just before the seat, on which the driver sits, just over the rump of the horse, and drives you from one part of the town to another at stated rates for a set-down; and a damned set-down it is sometimes, for you are well off if you are not set down in a kennel (gutter) by the breaking of the wheels, or an overset-down, nor can you see anything before you but your nod-nod-nodding charioteer, whose situation on the shafts obliges his motion to be conformed to that of the horse, from whence, I suppose, they have obtained the name of the Noddy.

For pleasure parties, or large groups heading off on a cockle-picking excursion to Sandymount the *chaise-marine* was preferred. This was a block-wheeled cart upon which the occupants sat with their feet dangling about six inches from the ground. The same foreign writer adds:

> Ten or a dozen will take one of these chaise-marines, and ride it by turns, the rate being seldom, in such cases, more

> than foot-pace. . . . I assure you, they are the drollest, merriest curricles you ever saw.

In the mid eighteenth century a small village known as 'Brickfield Town' stood on the site now occupied by Sandymount Green. It derived its name from the brickfields owned by Lord Merrion and stretching along the shore from there towards Merrion. The ground must have possessed good clay, as a too-sandy clay would have produced brittle and porous bricks, though the nearby sand and water were necessary for the 'slop-moulding'. By the early 1800s the drying hacks and the kilns of the brickmakers seem to have disappeared. By then Sandymount was coming into great favour as a watering place, complete with a fine hotel and a range of lodging houses built at the north-eastern side of the Green and continuous with Newgrove Avenue. Weston St John Joyce describes it thus:

> The extent to which it was patronised in consequence of its fine strand, pretty beach and depth of wave at full-tide, excited the ambition of the residents to make it an aristocratic resort, and in order to attain the desired degree of exclusiveness, the fee charged for bathing there was 2d., which, of course, restricted it to the nobility and gentry, the common people betaking themselves to Irishtown, where the fee was only 1d., and where there was a larger array of bathing boxes with plainer accommodation.

Scald Hill and Brickfield, ah, but what was the 'Conniving House', and where was it located? The Conniving House was a popular tavern which in former times stood where the present Seafort Avenue meets the Strand Road. The name immediately suggests to me a convenient meeting-place for smugglers and those 'law abiding' citizens who turned a blind eye, or connived, at the extensive trade in contraband for which the area was noted. We know, of course, that the belfry and vaults of nearby St Matthew's Church, Irishtown, (built for the seafaring community in 1703) were regularly utilised for storing contraband lace, kegs of brandy and claret and Rhenish wine hauled in at night by the local smugglers. By the by, an old salt in Dwyer's pub once told me that Irishtown and 'Raytown'

– to give Ringsend the nickname by which it is affectionately known to its denizens – are inhabited largely by the descendants of Devon and Cornish fishing families who sailed there to escape the attentions of the notorious Royal Navy 'press gangs' in the eighteenth century; this is an interesting connection, I think, because we also know that in Devon and Cornwall the vicarage cellars and church belfries traditionally provided the hiding places for the forbidden goods until the Preventative men and the Revenue and Coastguard cutters had gone elsewhere in their search for contraband.

Smugglers or no, the Conniving House seems to have been a jolly place. Thomas Amory (1692–1759) in his eccentric and fictionalised autobiography *The Life of John Buncle, Esq.*, gives us the following happy description of the inn:

> I set forward (1st May, 1725), and in five days arrived from the western extremity of Ireland at a village called Rings-end that lies on the Bay of Dublin. Three days I rested there, and at the Conniving House, and then got my horses on board a ship that was ready to sail, and bound for the land I was born in, I mean Old England . . . The Conniving House (as the gentlemen of Trinity called it in my time and long after) was a little publichouse, kept by Jack Macklean, about a quarter of a mile beyond Rings-end, on the top of the beach, within a few yards of the sea. Here we used to have the finest fish at all times; and in the season, green peas and all the most excellent vegetables. The ale here was always extra-ordinary, and everything the best; which with its delightful situation, rendered it a delightful place of a summer's evening. Many a delightful evening have I passed in this pretty thatched house with the famous Larry Grogan, who played on the bagpipes extremely well; dear Jack Lattin, matchless on the fiddle, and the most agreeable of companions . . . and many other delightful fellows who went in the days of their youth to the shades of eternity. When I think of them and their evening songs – *'We will go to Johnny Macklean's to try if his ale be good or not,'* &c., and that years and infirmities begin to oppress me, what is life!

I am a regular traveller to Sandymount, journeying there

by DART or bus. But there are times, too, when I permit that combination of imagination and a sense of history to convey me there by means of a jingling 'noddy', or, by linking arms with the happy cockle-pickers and letting my feet dangle a few inches from the ground, I travel by way of a slow-paced *chaise-marine*, 'the drollest, merriest curricle you ever saw'. Then, after a whole day on the sands, and with the evening breeze now scything in from the sea, I see myself drawn towards the echoing strains of Jack Lattin's fiddle.

I enter under a stone lintel and come into a dim place of tinted light. In a low-ceilinged tap-room whirls of tobacco smoke rise up to the blackened beams, the floors are freshly sawdusted and sand-strewn, the stairway short and stunted and creaking, with the fiddler Lattin seated on the lowest rung and the bagpiper Grogan a notch above him. In the wide grate of the inglenook a fire of coals and driftwood keeps a number of large iron pots simmering with a song of fish soups; from somewhere else the smell of warm oatcakes . . . and from the bar counter much laughter and song. There are times – only in my imagination, mind you – when I can almost taste Johnny Macklean's good ale.

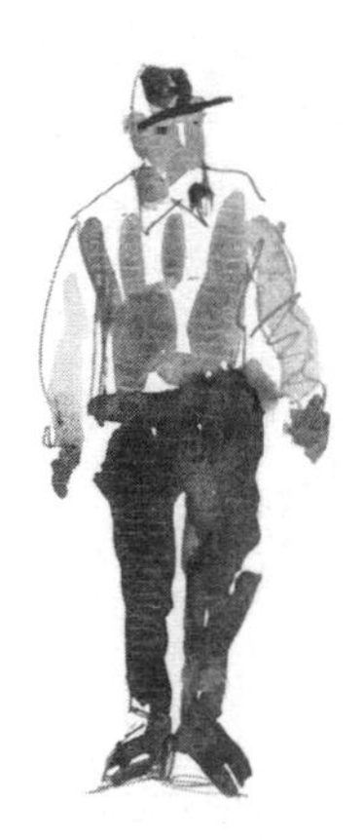

· 10 ·

Booterstown

THERE can be very few city areas in the world where one can pass so rapidly from leafy roadways hedged with honeysuckle to sudden views of the blue waters and dramatic sweep of Dublin Bay and still find oneself on the fringe of a fairly extensive wildlife sanctuary. That sanctuary is neatly tucked in between, on the one hand, the busy main road from the city centre to Dun Laoghaire and, on the other, one of the world's most modern high-technology electrified railways.

Booterstown Marsh is a nature reserve, one of the many roosting areas for thousands of birds using the mudflats of Dublin Bay as a source of food. Greater Dublin, in fact, is probably unique among the metropolitan districts of western Europe in that it includes within its boundaries two extensive wildlife sanctuaries, the Bull Island and Booterstown Marsh. The latter, with its mixture of fresh and salt water and its plashy muds, is an important wetland for many species of wildfowl and waders. It attracts all the main species. Their relentless foraging for the rich plant and animal life of this marsh tract is an inexhaustible mine for the patient bird-watcher and for the photographer. For the scribbler and the dreamer too . . .

I love Booterstown in the morning light when the Hill of Howth across the bay is still remote, blue and cloud-tipped and leaning against the dawn sky like something from an Italian postcard. And I love the little pools of dark brown water gathering in my heel marks, each slow, quiet footfall crushing out the rich and brackish smell of marshland, and all about me the unique example of the ageless mystery of migratory birds flourishing in the midst of early-morning traffic. At such times the marsh shares a timeless importance with all places in which generations of men and women have loved and toiled and made history, almost as if some part of their passion had soaked itself into the grass. It is strange, but human (and therefore a pardonable weakness), that so many of us should try to link ourselves to the past, to search for old tales and a half-remembered childhood even on a near-desolate and incongruous strip of fenland marooned in a city's environs.

At Booterstown archaeologists have found traces of the ancient double ditch constructed in pursuance of an Act of Poyning's Parliament in 1494 and which once delineated that curious defensive territory known as 'the Pale'. Some portions of the double ditch still existed right up until a century ago. Weston St John Joyce, at the time, identified that section known as 'from Merrion to the waters of the Dodder' as a kind of dyke running through the then fields south of Ailesbury Road from old Merrion churchyard to Seaview Terrace near Anglesea Bridge over the Dodder. The Pale was largely confined to the flat coastal plains stretching from the Dublin mountains in the south to the edges of Carlingford Lough in the north, and inside its protective bulwarks the early Norman settlers lived while keeping a wary eye on the Gaelic neighbours outside.

Immediately beyond the Pale were the hotly contested 'march lands', over which invader and native held sway at various times in the turbulent thirteenth and fourteenth centuries. The 'march lands' should not be confused with 'marsh lands'. The marches were boundaries, a kind of buffer zone between the Norman-held territories and those of the natives. The double ditch, or inner boundary, ran roughly parallel with the coastline from Dalkey to Donnybrook, then swung inland in a broad swathe to take in parts of Kildare, Meath and Louth, where it met the sea again at Dundalk.

To discourage any incursions of the Pale by such Gaelic marauders as the hardy Wicklow clansmen of the O'Byrnes and the O'Tooles, the Norman overlords built massive fortresses, like Merrion Castle, which once stood opposite the present DART rail crossing at Merrion Gates. One of the largest castles in County Dublin (and the ancestral home of the Fitzwilliam lords since the fifteenth century) the castle fell into decay in the early eighteenth century when its owners moved inland, and upwards, to Mount Merrion. It was partly dismantled in 1780, though its ruins were still evident on a map of 1820.

Why did the Fitzwillams quit their ancient castle and permit it to become a ruin? Well, for one thing the Wicklow raiders had finally been pacified. For another, it was a typical medieval fortress – a stout, graceless, uncomfortable chaos of stonework towers, dungeons and turrets, black with smoke, loud with clanking doors, shouts and sizzling fat and the yelp of hounds kicked away from the hearth. It was cold and draughty. It did not accord with the growing feeling for elegance in early Georgian Dublin. And besides, the Fitzwilliamses' aristocratic neighbours – the Fitzgeralds, Powerscourts, Cloncurrys and Ranelaghs – were building magnificent, non-military, neo-classical townhouses and country seats in the now tranquil lands of south County Dublin.

Tranquil? Well, not always. In Booterstown and Merrion there was for a while the awful problem of the marramounts, enough to drive anyone from even the most strongly fortified castle. What were the marramounts? *Walshe's Impartial Newsletter* of 16 May 1729 records the fearful news that:

> . . . A parcel of these outlandish marramounts which are called mountain rats, who are now here (in Booterstown and Merrion) grown very common, walk in droves and do a great deal of damage.

The *Newsletter* goes on to report that this strange, pestiferous breed of rodents are as large as 'cats and rabbits' and that the marramounts had devoured at least one child. I have been unable to trace the word marramount outside this one account from *Walshe's Impartial Newsletter*, but we do know that rats in time of famine, and pressed by hunger, will perform extensive migrations. During these migrations the whole swarm will cross considerable bodies of water, the rat being an expert swimmer.

So where did these hordes of marramounts come from: the nearby mountains after a bad winter? Or did they emerge from the many wrecks that littered the sands below Merrion Castle and whose skeletal masts peeped ominously above the surface of the tides beyond Booterstown? And how soon, or by what means, was the plague extirpated? The ancient authors, and even the Elizabethans – Ben Jonson, Sir Philip Sidney and Shakespeare – tell us that it was once a prevalent opinion amongst the Irish that rats in pasturage could be banished by means of rhyming verse or metrical charms and music. Shades of Bishop Hatto and the Pied Piper of Hamelin! Did the people of old Booterstown bombard the marramounts with a medley of rowdely-dowdely ballads?

And if it wasn't the marramounts, or a Georgian version of 'keeping up with the Joneses', which drove the Fitzwilliams from their ancient castle, might it have been Booterstown's reputation as being one of the most hazardous stretches of coastline near Dublin? It was a ship's graveyard; travellers' accounts written in the 1700s refer to the sea at Merrion and Booterstown as a tragic shore, littered with hulks and wrecks. Almost 400 people were drowned or dashed to pieces on the sharp rocks when the *Prince of Wales* and the *Rochdale* went down in a blinding snowstorm in November 1807. The weather-faded stone commemorating that tragedy may still be seen slumped against the wall of the old graveyard beside the present-day Tara Towers Hotel.

Highwaymen and road agents may possibly have been another reason why the Fitzwilliam magnates, 'lords of Merrion and all the lands adjoining thereto', decided to quit their ancestral home. The effete successors to the Earl of Pembroke – he who had wrested half a county from its warlike inhabitants with his sword! – had no real stomach for the nightly activities of the descendants of the dispossessed. The sequestered and tree-lined lanes skirting the fine mansions and leading to and from the 'celebrated sea-bathing places' of Booterstown and Blackrock was ideal territory for the daring highwayman. He came riding bravely into the rich land in search of rich pickings.

It was suspected that the seashore inns like the Conniving House at Irishtown, the Coach & Horse at Merrion and Jennet's Tavern at Blackrock were the haunts of smugglers and highwaymen. Had not the notorious Rock Road Gang taken over the Coach & Horse one evening, relieved the landlord of sixty pounds and then spent most of their booty buying drinks and toasting 'mine host' and the assembled company? And hadn't Jennet's Tavern proved to be something of a conniving house when the proprietor had to suddenly whisk his best-paying customers out of the taproom and secret them upstairs just half an hour before an angry Lord Ranelagh arrived to preside over an urgent meeting hastily convened to consider the most expeditious method of ridding the countryside around Booterstown of all highwaymen?

No doubt his lordship and the assembled gentlemen had a genuine grievance, but my feelings for the romance of Booterstown are such that I cannot quite visualise the local highwaymen as anything other than a breed of gallant adventurers. I see them – dressed in surtout and tricorn hat, their black masks not entirely concealing their handsome features – sighing mysteriously over a lady's gloved hand extended from the darkness of a halted carriage. Before rider and horse gallop off in a white slant of moonlight there is time for a merry compliment – what lady would not be happy to part with a bauble to such a charming thief? And was the immensely rich Lord Ranelagh any worse off for a lighter purse now and then? Perhaps the reality was much more grim. But for me the dispossessed rapparee and the highwayman will always be represented as brave, handsome, merciful, gallant to females, a hater of oppression; and if he robbed from the rich it was only to give large portions of the plunder to the poor.

Walsh's *Ireland Sixty Years Ago* gives us a glimpse of one such road agent, the Waterford rapparee and bandit William Crotty:

> Though well known personally to all the county, Crotty never hesitated to appear at fairs and markets, where he was generally well received. Like many other highwaymen he was in the habit of sharing with the poor what he plundered from the rich; and thus acquired popularity sufficient to procure him immediate warning of any danger which might threaten him. He frequented the fair green of Kilmacthomas, and openly joined with the young men in hurling and foot-ball on Sunday evenings, danced with the girls at wakes and patterns, and familiarly entered respectable houses. He once visited a lady, named Rogers,

> near Tramore, while she was entertaining a large company at dinner. The guests were terror-stricken when he walked into the room and displayed his arms; but he calmly desired a servant to give him the plate on the side-board, and his direction being instantly complied with, he walked out without committing any further depredation. The servant was immediately charged with being his accomplice, and threatened with prosecution; whereupon he ran after Crotty, and implored him to restore the plate. Crotty complied, returned to the house, and handed back the property to Mrs Rogers. She was profuse in her thanks, but he desired her to observe he was only lending the plate to her, and peremptorily demanded it back. She again surrendered it, and he said – 'Now, madam, remember it was you, and not your servant, who gave this to me, and do not charge him with the loss.' Such was the terror of his name that no attempt was made to pursue him.

There have been people unromantic enough to say that Dick Turpin didn't exist. Macaulay, I think, said as much, but it is too late now for an eminent historian to effect a reform in my thinking. One might as easily dispose of Robin Hood, King Arthur, Long John Silver or Santa Claus. Turpin's epic ride from Kilburn to York – over 200 miles! – still lives on. At York, Turpin's faithful mount, Black Bess, tottered, fell and finally expired. To have had such tales read to you, as a child, and at a parent's knee, is to be haunted by them forever.

Despite my liking for such accounts I have to admit that a great deal of the romance which has gathered like a halo round the names of Dick Turpin and Claude Duval in England, and around the names of Crotty, Collier, Shawn Crossach, Redmond O'Hanlon, Freney and Galloping Hogan in Ireland, is to be traced to fertile imaginations and to eighteenth- and nineteenth-century booksellers on the lookout for sensations. Indeed, so popular and successful were cheap books dealing with the exploits of highwaymen and knights of the road that at one time there seems to have been a positive fear that highway robbery would become the fashion. Gay's robust *Beggar's Opera* (1727) and the adventures of the fictitious Captain MacHeath were largely blamed for this spirit. At any rate, many a well-bred young gentleman had a turn at it for its excitement; and for those who were dispossessed or disinherited, disenchanted or down to their last penny, it was distinctly preferable to enlisting in the armies of the day. No wonder Lord Ranelagh and the gentry of Booterstown, Blackrock and Merrion were perturbed.

My mother first told me of Collier the Robber and how he daringly held up the northern mail-coach at Santry Woods. As a six-year-old schoolboy, and not far from mother's own childhood cottage, I was shown the mounting stone outside the door of the Boot Inn, where, as legend has it, the locals frequently hoisted a tipsy Jack Clinch into his saddle and then slapped the rump of his faithful horse and sent the highwayman galloping off to another adventure. At the time my mother told us that the Boot Inn was one of the oldest taverns in Ireland; dating from 1609 it had often, for over 300 years, been the nightly refuge for local rapparees, highwaymen, outlaws and rebels right up to the Civil War of 1922–23. Her people were all rooted in the land and lore of Fingal and the north county, and they knew every banshee hedge and haunted lane and most of the ballads associated with them. On that day she'd walked us up the Rathingle Road, past Snaid's Hill, to show us the brand-new aerodrome. Someone or something called Aer Lingus had just levelled out a couple of fields directly behind the Boot Inn and called it a 'runway'. They'd also erected a brand-new gleaming white building (said to be modelled on the style of the ocean-going liner *Queen Mary*'s top deck) and this was known as a 'terminal' building. The first aeroplane service from Ireland to England had commenced only four years earlier in 1936. To this day my mother still refers to the fields behind the Boot Inn as the 'Collinstown Cavalry Camp'. The rest of the world knows the sprawling, ever-expanding area as Dublin Airport. Highwaymen, headless coachmen, banshees and the remembered jingle of cavalry accoutrements as British troopers trotted down the main street of Swords in the years before the 1914–18 War are every bit as real to her as aeroplanes. Perhaps more so.

At the outset I said that my strolls about Dublin are a kind of persistent questing, a search for the identity of all

Dubliners, as it were, past and present. To explore one's childhood, and through it oneself, one's parents and one's mother town is always something of a mystery. And in the midst of such mysteries and explorations there are certain days that shine like jewels in the memory . . .

. . . I get off the train and take my bearings. In a moment or two I'm out on a pathway which, a century and a half ago, was a windswept causeway linking the mainland village of Booterstown to Ireland's first railway embankment. In those days the causeway was surrounded by sea water. Now the pathway is flanked by grassy marshland. I am less than four miles from the centre of Dublin and I am in the heart of a bird sanctuary.

Booterstown Marsh nestles or crouches with the air of pretending to be something else: a wild, boggy mountainside in the West maybe, or a tidal mudflat in Wexford. It is no such thing. Men have built and perfected their railroad and, beyond it, a broad highway, each hemming in the tract of tough, soggy grass and brackish water. Yet, here beside the DART rail line and the busy thoroughfare, wildfowl and waders, unconcerned and with perpetual optimism, search for nourishment, while I seek out a patch of firm, dry ground and gaze out at them.

I try to identify them. The curlew I know, with his streaky brown coat and his long, curved bill. And the black-and-white oyster catcher, and Brent geese. But those other ones – teal or lapwing or shoveler? I continue to watch, and wonder if the birds are aware of the smoke from my pipe going down the wind. The marsh is an open place. The wind blows always, even on a warm, placid day of sun. The grasses are ripe and dark and the wind is in them, pressing them back with gentleness. There is one brief, rare moment when the Rock Road is virtually free of traffic and there is no train rumbling by. The curlew's plaintive cry rings out in the stillness, pulling at my memory.

My father first brought us here by tram fifty years ago. He knew the names of all the birds. And trees. Grasses too, I shouldn't wonder. He had binoculars and a thick pocket-book full of coloured illustrations of the waders and wildfowl. In those far-off days I truly believed that he knew the name of every bird, wild animal, tree and plant, not only in County Dublin but throughout the entire world. For a Dublin barber he was a very well-read man. History. Poetry too:

> He shall not hear the bittern cry in the wild sky
> Where he is lain,
> Nor voices of the sweeter birds above the wailing
> Of the rain . . .

'Of course, lads', Da said, as he cast about for some dry hummock of sedge grass upon which we could sit, and at the same time withdrawing the big thermos flask from his bag, 'it's very unlikely that either Thomas McDonagh or Francis Ledwidge could have actually heard the bittern's cry in their lifetime. You see, the bittern hasn't bred in this part of the world since the 1840s, or thereabouts. Since the beginning of this century it occurs only as a very occasional visitor.'

He poured steaming hot tea from the flask into our mugs, tea that was almost the colour of the marshy pools surrounding our little island of grass. As he unwrapped the big flat sandwiches prepared by Ma earlier that morning he added: 'And there's another thing, the bittern doesn't really cry. From all accounts it makes a deep "booming" sound. So there . . .'

The sandwiches were laid out neatly on the surface of his canvas bag.

'Still, bittern or booming, it makes no difference to a fine poem. Always remember that, lads; inaccuracy is no harm in poetry and it is by no means the worst of conversational or writing faults. As long as what has to be said is sound in heart and catches the right mood, that's the thing. Always remember that. Careful now, that tea is scalding hot . . .'

Is that where it all began, where the decision was made, consciously or unconsciously? My father's words had an instant appeal to a seven-year-old dunce who could grasp nothing of the cold logic or the accuracy required for such complexities as long division, multiplication or geometry. But poetry and writing? That might be something else. Here waited the romance of old tales, of highwaymen and pirates and beautiful princesses, all lurking in the pages of the many books on our parents' shelves – stories that were sound in heart and caught the right mood – and which lay in friendly ambush, ready to leap out and capture a schoolboy's imagination. Might I not study such tales with more success than arithmetic?

I think I may have made my decision to become a scribbler of sorts that long-ago day on Booterstown Marsh.

A blizzard of birds comes swirling in from seaward. Dunlin? I don't know. But my father would have known, would have estimated their number to the nearest score, I think. The shadows lengthen, the sun sinks and the little marshland changes its colour. Its grasses sway back before the breeze. The smooth, dark stems shine in the dying light. Time to go . . .